Survival of the Prepared

Volume I
Preparation prior to an
Emergency or Disaster

*An informational guide to give you
and your family the best possible
chance at surviving an emergency
or disaster*

L.F. Wesseln

Survival of the Prepared

Volume I
Preparation prior to an Emergency or Disaster

L.F. Wesseln

"If money is your hope for independence you will never have it. The only real security that a man will have in this world is a reserve of knowledge, experience, and ability."
-Henry Ford

Table of Content

Chapter Six

Chapter Seven

Chapter Eight

Bread	Hard Cider
Butter	Jerky
Brine	Lard, Render
Campfire	Pemmican
Candles	Solar Box Oven
Candle Wicks	Sourdough Starter
Ferment, Lacto-	Sprouts
Fire sticks	Whey
Glue	Yogurt

Chapter Nine

"Be Prepared... the meaning of the motto is that a scout must prepare himself by previous thinking out and practicing how to act on any accident or emergency so that he is never taken by surprise."
-Robert Baden-Powell

Note from the Author –

My child saw me sitting by the computer and asked if I was working on my survivaling book. I answered yes, then corrected her saying there is no such word, its either surviving or survival. But after a moment I figured, why not? It's what I do. I actively put survival into practice by gathering, storing, learning, educating and fine tuning my own ability to survive the *surviving*... in survival. Hence the word: survivaling.

Once you start to see how dependent we all are on technology, right down to the infrastructure of this and all great nations, you will come to the undeniable conclusion that we are sitting on the edge. The smallest glitch can cause this world to fall to its knees. When this truth becomes apparent, you will most likely find yourself ready to embrace 'survivaling'.

This book has been put together especially for you. You were either drawn to it, or someone gave it to you, for a reason; survival is hardwired in the human heart and mind. It is instinct to do whatever it takes to survive. But just as animals become domesticated so we have also. The journey back to self reliance and preservation is not overly dramatic or scary; it is just a learned response to what we already know in our heads and hearts.

There is information throughout the pages that contain interesting points that may reinforce what you already know or a facts that you were unaware, whatever your thoughts are on the subject go ahead and write it down in this book.

There is extra room for your personal information or thoughts; add your own story and give it to the next generation.

If you do not like certain portions, simply disregard it or put a big line through it. The biggest request I have is to please implement some kind of plan, whatever pulls at your heart to do, do it.

I'd like to give a special thank you to my 'survivaling' family and friends for their patience and love. To Dan, Dale and the late Mark Barnes for spurring me on to write all of this down, to Kristen, who has a love for books and talks with me about conspiracy theories and end of days scenarios (fun stuff!).

Thank you to Lenae, Ken, Thomas and Kristen for putting their lives on the line in the military, serving this great nation. And of course, to God Almighty, for without His guidance and blessing of insight and patience I would not be writing this.

Thank You, Thank You, Thank You.

L.F Wesseln

"Books serve to show a man that those original thoughts of his aren't very new at all."
-Abraham Lincoln

Chapter One

Life as we know it...

Living in North America, we have become complacent and used to having an "easy" life; indoor plumbing and toilets are considered normal. As our culture grew, our society changed, and we have adapted and grown to know this way of life. We forget that gardening, hunting, trapping, tanning hide, making things like soap, candles and butter, even sewing our own clothes was a way of life only 100 years ago.

In the good 'ole days grandpa would take his grandchildren out fishing. He would teach them how to tie knots, dig up night crawlers and cast a line. Grandma would jar or can the vegetables from the backyard garden. Life was harder back then but life's lessons were passed on from generation to generation; the families' legacy was preserved.

"Pain is inevitable. Suffering is optional"
- Anony-mouse

Now we rely almost entirely on the transportation industry to bring food and supplies to our local stores, where we can leisurely go to purchase anything we wish. We have forgotten how to take care of our own basic needs.

We are all aware of the potentials of an emergency and/or disaster happening, whether man made or natural, and have seen the results of disruptions to our supplies. For the past few years our society has taken a turn towards hard times; the economy has gone up and down like a roller coaster.

All countries throughout history, no matter what social order or economic state, have experienced fluctuations in their economy. A country's economic changes are often affected by severe weather, war, religion, government policies and its people. Are we any different than ancient empires when it comes to the possibility of our great nation falling into chaos and ruin?

Some people are very aware of what is going on with their own economic hardships, the delicate global economy and world politics. They see the world changing and are sure that 'it' will happen soon; whatever 'it' may be. They are the **prepared**; having every kind of supply and skill ready. Then, there are the knowledgeable ones who are also procrastinators, they will be caught off guard but will be the first to say "I saw this coming". And then there are people who have no clue of what may happen nor do they want one. Those people are the ones that will be standing with their hands out for food, shelter and comfort. They will expect to be saved by the government, and they will expect it to be quick. The problem with that approach is that when the help comes, it may not be quick, if help comes at all.

Just look at recent history; hurricane Katrina, the earthquake and tsunami in Japan, etc. The slow response to disaster areas is not because governments and charities are slow to respond (relatively speaking) but because it takes time to get anywhere when the areas infrastructure has been affected.

In light of these events it is strange that some people are *anti-preparation*. They make fun of individuals who prepare for the worst, saying the 'preppers' are paranoid or are conspiracy theorist. They do not look at the situation logically. There are mandatory earthquake and fire drills in schools, you cannot go on a cruise without going through the 45 minute lifeboat drill or take a flight without listening to the emergency landing procedures, they now give emergency evacuation directions at theaters before the movie starts. All this is considered smart, not paranoid. Those same people who bock at your preparedness have a smoke detector in their home and a spare tire in the car, all as a precaution against the unexpected happening.

You *will* have something unexpected happen in your life, therefore, it should be prepared for as 'expected'.

Once something does happen, survival supplies may only be available to a small group of people, thus leaving a very large group of people that are desperately waiting on somebody else to come recue them to go without any supply. Some people, I would venture to say most, out of necessity, would resort to violence to get whatever they want or need. In order to stay safe from these people, you will need to learn about personal protection and avoidance.

Any way you look at the future, concerns that need to be addressed and preparations that need to be implemented are described in four areas, they are

- Emergency/Disaster Preparation for a short term event
- Emergency/Disaster Preparation for a long term event
- Evacuation Preparation
- Survival Skills - The "How to…"

Becoming a 'Prepper', so to speak

Being prepared starts with the understanding of the need to be ready for life's unpredictable events. There does not need to be over the top fear or a threat of imminent danger to make one a 'Prepper'; it starts with the simple need to be safe and secure.

When and not if, an emergency happens, will you be ready? With the threats of terrorist attack, natural disaster, pandemic, economic collapse or personal financial hard times, you need to have a survival plan in place. In a disaster/emergency, five things affect if you survive or not:

- Location - where you live and work
- Preparation – supplies
- Knowledge – skills
- Attitude – can do attitude and will to live
- Luck - call it what you will - right place right time

We're living in precarious times ... and the unprepared may not survive.

The very best thing that a 'survival' minded person can do, after preparing for themselves and their family, is to *associate themselves with other like minded and skilled survivalists.* There is strength in numbers. The group should have a leader. This chosen leader does not have to *know* everything but should have the ability to lead people and delegate responsibilities. The day will come when everyone's *true* character will emerge when a disaster happens.

The people in your group need to be trustworthy and dependable. When a new potential 'member' is to join, everyone in the group must agree. No one else should know of your food and survival supply, not even your children; since little ones will say things to casual acquaintances that will remember the conversation when the time arrives and they are without food. Only the people you choose should have the knowledge of what you are doing.

Being prepared does *not* have to alter your life.

There are expert survivalists that really push for a retreat home in the wilderness, a fully stocked compound and becoming the aggressor. But in all seriousness, if you spend your time looking for trouble in troubled times - you will find it and most likely will not survive the encounter. Protect yourself and family by all means. Lead, if you are able. But most importantly, be part of the solution and not the problem.

If you wish to go deeper in your knowledge and skills about the survival lifestyle, *Survival of the Prepared Volume II* goes into partial and total sustainability and off grid living. How deep you want to go is up to you. Learning the method of canning, dehydrating and sun drying food will extend your ability to have different kinds of foods year-round. Steam pressure canning, bread makers, freezers, sealers and sewing machines all use electricity. Learning to make things and preserve food without the use of electricity will be rewarding and beneficial if the time comes when electricity is not available.

Remember, supply can only do so much. If the disaster is flooding or fire, volcano ash or anything else that will make getting to your supply difficult or even ruin your supply, you can still survive. The 'how to do something' skills are right up there with water in importance.

Your survival will depend upon thinking on your feet, knowledge and 'street smarts '. The more you know and practice, the better the quality of your life will be during *and* after the emergency or disaster hits.

Quick test...BAM *something* happened! Big or small, who knows – no one knows what is going on, no phone, and no electricity. Are you ready as of right this second? MOST LIKELY...NO. But, right now taking the time to research, you are on your way to *not* worrying when something does happen.

Answer these simple questions to see just how ready you truly are for the 'unexpected'. Then take the test over again in a few weeks and then again in a few months. See what you still need to work on and what has already been addressed.

How ready are you for an emergency?

- ❏ My computer is backed up frequently and backups are also stored off site
- ❏ I know the type of emergency/disaster that is most likely to occur in my local area
- ❏ My family knows which in and out of town friend or relative to contact in the case of an emergency
- ❏ If communication systems are down or off grid, all family members know where to meet as a 1st/2nd choice
- ❏ Each family member can quickly find their personal flashlight with fully charged batteries
- ❏ The location of the fire extinguisher and how it is used is known by each family member
- ❏ I have first aid supplies including extra prescriptions, contact lenses, etc
- ❏ I have an alternate source of heat if the power fails or the furnace does not work
- ❏ I always either wear comfortable walking shoes or have them at work or in my car
- ❏ I have an emergency kit/bag ready to grab if I need to leave my home quickly
- ❏ There is stored water for each family member at 1 gallon a day times X amount of days
- ❏ I have vet records and an extra supply of food and water for each of my pets
- ❏ I know where the electricity and gas shut off is located in my house/apartment
- ❏ If timed, I could secure my home and evacuate in less than 5 minutes
- ❏ I have discussed emergency preparedness with those whom I trust and can count on
- ❏ I have a means of protection for me and my family (gun, knife, pepper spray etc.)
- ❏ I have enough supplies to be self sufficient for at least 14 days or more

Write what you need to do here.

Chapter Two

Where to start

After taking the 'How ready are you for an emergency?' test, you have an idea of your level of preparation. Now, take the steps needed to get you where you want to be; have fun on your journey, take family and friends that you *trust* along for the ride.

There will be 'To Buy' lists and 'To Do' lists to choose from, some of the lists will have items that overlap each other. Decide if the item needs to be doubled. Look over the lists then decide if you want to do all of them at once, one at a time or none at all … it's up to you.

You will need to take inventory of what you *have*, what you *know*, what you will need to *buy* and finally what you need to *learn*.

Start by doing something; anything, but do *something*.

> *"In business or in football, it takes a lot of unspectacular preparation to produce spectacular results."* –
> ***Roger Staubach,***
> ***Hall of Fame Football Player***

Short Term Emergency/ Disaster Preparations List

Short term emergencies and/or disasters are just that, short in the amount of time there is an upset in normal daily activities. It could mean a flat tire or something extremely serious and bit more local like a small earthquake, hurricane or small tornado. The shortness of time in recovering depends on the size of the disaster. Unless your area was completely demolished, most services are restored in a few days or weeks. So, by this definition, short term may or may not be costly and detrimental.

This list is for the short or slightly disruptive type disaster; which generally can be dealt with easily, and life as we know it goes right back to 'life as we know it'.

Personal Information Protection

The very first thing to do is protect your personal information. Is your computer backed up on a separate external drive and an offsite (i.e. online) backup location? If not, you are at risk of losing everything and should choose a backup method immediately. There are numerous web sites and providers that will make the process of saving and recovering your information easy - for a nominal fee.

Along with digital backup, you will need to have your important and irreplaceable papers combined for easy access and portability. Place all vital information in an Emergency Binder. The Emergency Binder List is in the back of the book along with the Evacuation Grab List.

Where to Put Your Supply

Before you start to gather a supply of food and non-food items, you will need to figure out where you are going to put your supply. Basements are great; they stay cool and usually at a constant temperature. If it is possible, close the heating duct to the storage area.

Garages are ok for non-food items but the heat and cold are too extreme for food storage. Garage storage should be in the back area so that it is not easily seen when the garage door is open. You do not want the outside world to see all your supply; you may become an easy target. Spare rooms and closets are good places too, but you do have to be organized and remember what you have and where everything is placed. Start to clear an area and label shelves, bins, totes and containers. You will need strong shelves. The type of shelf is up to you but the stronger the better because of the weight of the food and water. A one-gallon jug of water weighs a little bit more than 8 lbs.

Water

Start collecting soda liter bottles, juice bottles and water gallons to create water storage. Do not to use milk gallons because even after a good cleaning there may be residual microbials left behind which will grow and contaminate the water. However, if you have a large amount of milk gallon jugs, by all means use them for non-potable water use (washing clothes, etc).

For containers, you can find some pretty good deals in the camping section of your local store. Also check container web sites, just remember that they need to be food grade.

You will need quite a few of these small containers to get the recommended amount of water - so it may be wise to get a 55 gallon water barrel. You can opt for a 35, 55 even 100-gallon barrel that come with a spout and faucet. These are great if you have no intention of moving the barrel and they are compact in comparison to the many bottles that you will need to gather and store. The plastic storage tanks can be left outside but beware of the frozen water cracking the plastic.

Viruses, bacteria and some protozoa, that are human parasites, cause diseases. Some protozoa parasites are found in the soil and water. Examples of human diseases caused by protozoa:

- Malaria
- Amoebiasis
- Giardiasis
- Toxoplasmosis
- Cryptosporidiosis
- Trichomoniasis
- Chagas disease
- Leishmaniasis
- Dysentery

There are three methods of disinfecting water: chemical, boiling and reverse osmosis. But, upon filling the storage containers with regular tap water you will not need to do anything to condition the water, it is already considered pure. Change the water every year or so to keep the water as fresh as possible.

However, if you are gathering water from a river, lake or somewhere in nature you will have to purify the water by using either the chemical or boiling method.

A few drops of non-scented bleach (5.25%– 6% Sodium Hypochlorite) 30 minutes before consumption will kill bacteria and viruses but not protozoa. To gauge bleach amount use this basic rule of thumb, for every quart use two drops of bleach, 1 gallon = 8 - 16 drops. Open the water container and let it air out for at least 30 minutes before drinking. If the water still has a strong bleach smell allow more time before consuming. If the water does not have a slight bleach odor, repeat the smaller dosage and let stand another 15 minutes. A scant scent is fine and drinkable.

Iodine is the second chemical used for water purification. Iodine has been proven effective in killing off viruses, bacteria and protozoa. However, the colder the water is, the more time it will take to purify with iodine. The iodine flavor is not pleasing at all. The best way to avoid this is to not use this method.

All *gathered* water should be boiled before drinking. Bring to a hard boil for 1 minute – anything longer wastes water, anything shorter does not kill microorganisms. Boiling is by far the best way to disinfect water. This method kills most everything but does not remove radioactive materials. Let the water cool before using.

The water needed for survival is one gallon per person per day. The generally accepted time for a short term emergency is up to 14 days. So, for a family of 4 that will equal out to 56 gallons of stored drinkable water. But, as everyone knows, emergencies are not always tied up in nice little time frames as two weeks. If you feel the need to gather more water - please do so.

If the emergency hits and you do not have enough stored water, your home has a number of places where you can find emergency water.

- **Hot Water Heater Tank** – open valve and drain into clean bucket
- **Canned Goods** – Tuna, canned vegetables, beans and fruit all contain liquids that can be drained and consumed.
- **Pipes** -If you live in a multilevel home, you can drain the water in your pipes by using gravity to your advantage. After the water lines into your house have been shut off, drain your pipes by using the lowest faucet in your house.
- **Toilet Water** – In an emergency you can gather the water from the flush tank (not the bowl) of your toilet. Only use this water as a last resort and only if you are sure it is free of chemicals.
- **Rainwater** - Use large pots and containers to catch and store rainwater. Use a tarp to collect the rain by hanging a tarp with one side higher than the other and down to a point where the water is funneled into a barrel. You can cut up a tarp and use it for the collection of water. Fasten all sides and corners level, weigh down the center with a stone and cut very small slits in the tarp so the water can then drain into a large open mouth barrel sitting under the lowest point. The water collected from rain and snow is considered clean *if* it has not come into contact with anything else, like the roof, gutter or down spout. If you gather the water in a barrel from a gutter spout the water then has the rinsed off roof dirt. Let the dirt settle to the bottom of the barrel, ladle the water off the top, filter through cloth or coffee filter then boil.

Food

Most people's food pantry is three days away from empty. While water may be more critical in a survival scenario and you *may* be able to survive a few weeks or even months without food; you will become weak, dizzy, susceptible to illnesses, and unable to perform survival-related tasks. You will need every ounce of energy to stay out of harm's way.

The two-week food storage list should be extensive and personalized to you and your family. This is where you sit down with your family (if you wish) and discuss the meals you eat on a regular basis. Write down *everything*. Include spices and condiments. This is the beginning of *your* food storage list.

Start with a 2-week list. After that, you double the list. This is approximately your one-month list. Then double it again and then again. This will be your 1-month, 3 months and 6-month list and then the eventual goal of a year supply. Think nonperishable foods. i.e.: canned meat, vegetables, stew, sloppy Joe mix, spaghetti sauce, fruit cocktail, fruit juice and anything else you like. If you have a special meal that you eat once in a while, add that in for variety. Try new recipes. Add in desserts and treats. Nothing lifts moral or brings back the 'normal' like comfort foods.

If you do decide to go for the 'full year' it may take more than a year's amount of time to get everything needed. Continue to purchase one or two extra pieces for your supply, *every* time you go shopping. If you normally buy one or two bags of noodles…this time, buy three or four. Then the next time, buy the extra spaghetti sauce.

Try buying bulk item on sale and splitting them into smaller usable portions. Also splitting the cost with a fellow survivalist makes very sound economical sense.

You will see your shelves get full and may be tempted to not go grocery shopping again for a few weeks. But by using the supply on hand you will not be building up a food supply but consuming it. Tempting as this seems, stay focused on building your supply. It is also tempting to just put the food away and forget about it; the key is to rotate the food. First bought should be the first used. By rotating through the food you have in your storage your food supply stays fresh. No one wants to see expiration dates come and go on the food supply they spent money and time building.

Heat

Alternative heat and warmth will need to be addressed, this does not seem to be a big deal in the middle of summer but in the dead of winter, a nice fireplace comes in handy. A potbelly stove or pellet stove also works to heat up the living room or kitchen area. Most deaths in winter time emergencies are from carbon monoxide poisoning, so proper ventilation is essential.

Get a good firewood supply and know where you can get more wood when needed. Remember that everyone else who is without wood will be after the wood supply you thought was available to you. Get your supply now. An alternative heat source is a necessity for cooking. You can bake meals in a solar oven (See 'How to make a Solar Oven') or cook over a wood-burning fireplace, use an outdoor grill or fire pit.

Because you do not know how long the electricity will be out, double or triple your propane supply.

The recommended cook wear is cast-iron. It is heavy so it retains its heat and cooks evenly. It will not die after multiple uses over the extreme heat of direct fire, as other pots and pans will not last. Cast iron needs to be coated with oil before use so it becomes black and obtains its non-stick properties. Do not use soap to wash it, as it will lose its seasoned-ness. This is another advantage of cast iron if soap is not abundant. (See "How to make soap')

Light

Essential items are a flashlight, a lantern and plenty of replacement or (solar power) rechargeable batteries. Candles help light up a room but are a potential fire hazard and need to be watched. The candles can break the glass container they're in or drip or knock over. (See "How to make Candles") Just be smart about it and you will be fine.

An oil lamp will burn clean for hours but if you do not have one – a cooking-oil lamp can be made with simple items from around the house; to improvise use a clear glass jar that will not tip easily, cooking oil, twisted cotton string for wicks and an uncurled paperclip to hold up the wick in place. Once lit, it can last for hours. This makeshift lantern is ideal for short term events but cooking oil is too valuable for cooking and baking food to waste it as a light fuel source *if* the event goes long term. Buy a few oil lamps along with extra fuel and you will be set.
Collect matches and lighters, store them in a moisture-proof jar. They are inexpensive so get a lot! Multiply the paper matches by cutting them length-wise in half. Practice now so you won't waste later.

First Aid Kit and Medical Supplies

Can you just imagine what it would be like if the electrical grid was down, hard line phones and cell towers did not work -- no communication, no 911, no fire department, no police, no ambulance? This scenario is scary enough, now add an injury - with no disinfectant or bandages; you will see how a first aid kit is invaluable.

Purchase or gather items for a well-stocked medical first aid kit. Now add to that sutures, surgical instruments and antibiotics and we're taking self sufficiency when medical personal are not readily available. Make sure all your prescription medications should have a back up supply. Rotate through the meds to make sure everything stays current and within expiration dates.

Take a CPR class and get caught up on the basic life support procedures. Remember, this is for short-term emergency preparation but what is short? One day with a sliced finger? It could get infected. Two days with a broken bone? How about 5? 10? 14?

Clothing

Make sure that in the off season your cold-weather boots, overshoes, raincoats, ponchos and warm clothing, even in summer, are accessible. After an emergency, these would become unobtainable. Also have outside work clothes and work shoes ready. Work gloves are on another list and should be a priority.

Sleeping

Gather a couple of sleeping bags or blankets and pillows per person. If it's cold shared body heat works very well. If you are at home, everything stays pretty much 'normal' but you may want to all sleep in the room with the fireplace to keep warm.

If you are forced to evacuate bring all you can carry. It might be a hard surface where you will have to lay your head. Keep all bedding as clean as possible as washing will be very difficult in a disaster scenario. Sleeping bags will keep cleaner on the inside longer than loose blankets.

Sanitation

Along with the essentials of food and water, shelter, warmth and light there is the need for sanitation. Without this essential need being addressed - all sorts of disgusting problems occur; disease crops up where there was none before. Keeping clean is important.

If the electrical grid is down sewer-pumping stations will not be operational. Sewer or water mains may break during a disaster. Even if water is available, local authorities may ask you not to flush toilets; the water may be needed for fighting fires.

Toilets that should not or cannot be flushed can still be used. After the water is emptied from the toilet bowl, place a plastic bag over the toilet opening. When finished using, add a small amount of deodorant or disinfectant to the bag. The plastic bag is then wrapped tight with a knot and stored away from the other trash. After taking the plastic bag off, place a new one over the bowl for the next person.

Keep on hand a large supply of heavy duty plastic bags and at least one extra-large garbage can with a tight fitting cover. This garbage can should have paper placed on the bottom, lined with a heavy duty garbage bag and used solely for emergency storage of bags containing excrement and urine until the sewage system is back online, or until other long term arrangements can be made.

If you live in an apartment, you may not have room to keep a large garbage can. If that is the case, use multiple smaller covered pails.

Another way is to dig a cat-hole, as you would if you were out in the wilderness camping. It is a small hole dug in the ground in which feces is deposited. The topsoil where the enzymes break down human waste is only in the *top* 6 inches of soil. This hole should not be near a water source and at least 50 feet from living quarters. Once you are finished, cover the hole with dirt.

Untreated raw sewage can pollute fresh ground water supplies. It also attracts flies and promotes the spread of diseases.

If there is a baby in the house, it is best to keep an ample supply of disposable diapers. But in an emergency/disaster you may run out of diapers. Any moisture resistant material can be cut and folded to diaper size and lined with absorbent material. It will not be the most comfortable but it will work in a pinch. Wrap up and throw away the soiled material in the human waste garbage can.

The extra needed supplies are toilet tissue, sanitary napkins and at least 2 gallons of household bleach solution should be kept on hand for disinfecting purposes.

If the emergency/disaster last longer than a few days then a long-term solution has to be addressed. A latrine and/or outhouse should be built as soon as possible. A makeshift latrine is just a cat-hole three or four feet long and six inches deep. No more than 5 people should use it for no longer than 3 days. At that point, it should be buried completely and another one dug. Let a week or more go by before that spot can be used again. All precautions should be addressed; 50 feet from water source and living quarters, etc.

Security

Last, but not least, is you and your family's security. The first part is to make you NOT a target. That would include making your efforts invisible to the rest of the world. It is important that you keep your supply out of sight and your work *not* known by your neighbors. Only the people in your core group will have knowledge of your efforts. The reason for this is that when an emergency or disaster happens, *you* can decide who and how to help your neighbors and friends.

If everyone knows that you have a large inventory of food, there will be people standing at your door looking for a handout. You will have your heartstrings pulled to the breaking point and your supply greatly reduced.

There are those who are kind hearted and will ask for help ...then there are those who will not hesitate to *take* what they want. A disaster will bring out the very best in people and will drudge up the very worst in people. There are a lot of **bad** people out there and with little or no police and therefore law enforcement to keep them in line; they will hurt those that are easy targets. Do *not* make yourself a target.

If you have to walk long distances try to do so during the time of day or night that is best for that area – city vs. country. Try to have a buddy system in place. Never walk alone if you can help it. Wear dark uneventful clothes; keep yourself uninviting to attackers. Be very aware of your surroundings. Keep chitchat to a minimum. Keep eyes moving and look for the unexpected. Think 'covert'. Keep your head up but do not make eye contact with anyone until you are safe.

As you walk use walls and/or outcroppings to stand behind while gauging the next steps to the next stopping point. Keep your line of sight clear and avoid choke points and bottlenecks. Have a map of the area with you always. Remember where you are at all times and where you are going.

> *Anakin Skywalker*: How did you know they wouldn't just attack us?
> *Obi-Wan Kenobi*: Because I make observations while you think with your lightsaber."
> **Star Wars**

The second part of security is the actual use of weapons and self defense. The key is balance. Balance in your thinking and behavior. Know yourself enough to know what you can and cannot do. Do not be afraid to hurt someone physically-- if they are a threat. Most people act timidly when fighting because they don't want to hurt someone else. Understandable! But know this; the ones coming at you are very willing to *hurt* you. Do <u>not</u> hesitate. Practice the motion of your hands and feet. This will serve as a muscle reminder when the time comes to actually use your own body as a weapon. Take a self defense class; be aggressive in your own defense.

Buy yourself a gun and learn how to use it if you have not done so already. There are always debates on the best kind but it all comes down to what you are comfortable using. Ask around, talk to salesman, hunters, and friends. Really educate yourself before you purchase anything.

There are many different kinds and sizes of weaponry. Handguns are easier to carry but more expensive and are not the best for hunting larger animals. They are great for personal defense. Rifles are the best choice for hunting large and small game.

A shotgun is simple and effective. A very strong deterrent from would-be thieves is the sound of a pump action shotgun being readied. After reading that sentence your imagination kicked in and you heard the sound, didn't you? Now that's a definite deterrent.

A shotgun and rifle do not have to be registered with the government. Private purchases are still legal in certain states so check with local authorizes for regulations.

Which one is better, a pistol or revolver? That is up to your personal likes and dislikes. What feels right in your hand? The grip, weight, recoil or kick, style and cost each factor in on which gun you will own.
What about a Shotgun? Or rifle? Why not have all three!? They each have a special role.

Buy with cash and do not sign a bill of sale; this will leave a paper trail and lead right back to you, if there ever comes a day that the government decides to come take away our rights to bear arms. You might say that can never happen to us since the Second Amendment reads:

"A well regulated militia being necessary to the security of a Free State, the right of the People to keep and bear arms shall not be infringed."

Laws can be changed by a power hungry government. But, by adding more restrictions and gun bans to law abiding citizens then only the unlawful will own guns.

Before any more restrictions can be placed on the law books it is a really good idea to get a gun and ammo. It is better to be safe than sorry. Be responsible and have all the needed precautions in place when dealing with guns and ammo. A concealed handgun carry class is great for learning the fundamentals of firearm handling, care and laws. Buy a gun safe or case and a large amount of ammo *now* since prices are going up and the caliber you need may not be available later.

If in the event your environment gets so bad that you are caught in a life or death situation and you or your family are threatened -- if you do *not* feel you can shoot someone -- carry a can of mace or pepper spray.

This will allow you a few extra seconds to get away. Do not carry a gun if you have no intention of using it; *it will be taken away from you by force.*

Practice at the shooting range and be on the lookout for training opportunities in your area. Just remember it is not all about combat, military tactics and weapons. These skills are great and fun, but in reality you are more likely to need to know how to splint a broken leg, bake bread, purify water or track game, than how to set up an ambush or take out a tank.

Start Prepping Now

Now that you have the list of what to do-- it's important that you get something done right away. If you have the means to buy all of the supply at one time –great—but if you are like most people -- going at this step by step is more conducive. In any and every case -- doing *something* can help you be one step closer to self sufficiency. You will get excited when you see your supply area and skills start to develop.

Go back and review as often as you need. Add your thoughts along the edges and open spaces. This will keep you involved and motivated.

The old cliché "Better late than never" does not apply here. Doing something now is better than leaving it until later and later never coming. Or "later" comes too soon and finds you wanting.

"Never leave that till tomorrow which you can do today."
- Benjamin Franklin

Chapter Three

Food and Non-Food Lists

Here are lists of foods and non-food items. Every time you go to the store for groceries or a quick run to get milk, pick up a little something extra. For example, when you go to the gas station pick up a few lighters and matches. Grocery shopping – get toilet paper every time. Bleach (for disinfecting water) is pretty cheap if you are tight on money that week. Do not forget your favorite spices if not on the list.

The Food List contains 60 different basic food items. However, also purchase some snack foods and powdered drink mixes. Stock up on Tang and Lemonade, Coffee, Tea, Soft Drinks, Beer and Wine. Some of those powders and mixes are considered junk with little or no nutritious value but can help relieve the boredom of drinking plain water.

"You cannot be disciplined in great things and indiscipline in small things.
-General George S. Patton Jr.

The larger packages are usually a little cheaper per ounce, but half the package may spoil after you open it and before it can be all used; find ideas on preserving your unused portion in the "Preserving Fresh Fruit and Vegetables" section.

It is a good idea to purchase food in more than one food category at a time so if a disaster were to occur before you are finished building your total supply, you would have a smaller supply in *each* major food group. Try to keep the supply balanced with the same amounts of meat, vegetables, fruit and grains. Dairy products are not mandatory for health but a large amount of calcium comes from dairy. Adjust the quantities based on your family's actual needs. If family members drink a lot of milk, then you should purchase more dry powdered milk than suggested.

It is very easy to forget what you have already purchased, keep a written list of all the items you have added to your reserves. This list will help you to strategically build your food stores without overlooking something or buying too much of something else. Most people skip this step and just wing it. If your storehouse is orderly and easily seen, then everything that is needed is recognizable. But, if things are placed in white super pails or cans that are not clearly marked or just thrown on a shelf - then a clipboard with a running inventory works well.

Ask a lot of questions.
"How can I make this as easy as possible?"
"How much extra money can I afford each week or month to dedicate to prepping?"
"What is next on my list?"

Basics and Bare Minimum Essentials Food List

It is recommended to always start your food storage program by storing the basics. This should be your starting point.

- Grains
- Legumes
- Dry milk
- Sugar and honey
- Salt
- Oil
- Garden Seed Bank

These have come to be known as the basics or bare essentials. Including the garden seed on the list is a way to grow your own food for the future. Do not underestimate the power these foods, as they have been shown throughout history to sustain life. It is important to know how to prepare and use these basics essentials. Wheat alone will do no good if you do not have other baking items necessary to make edible food out of it. Now add foods from the extended list and you will have the foundation for a well rounded food supply.

The standard three month emergency food supply list is for a family with two average American adults and two children. Or this list can be for one adult for a full year. The list does not take into account the calories or nutritional values needed for each family member.

Extended Basic Food List

- Water – 1 gallon per person per day OR a way to disinfect a water source
- Wheat berries – hard white and hard red
- Salt
- Shortening or Oil
- Dry Instant Milk
- Powdered Eggs
- Honey and/or Sugar
- Flour
- Yeast
- Baking Powder
- Baking Soda
- Cream of Tarter
- Tomatoes – Canned, whole, sliced, diced and stewed
- Powdered Butter
- Powdered Cheese
- Flavoured and Unflavoured Gelatin
- Canned Milk, condensed and sweetened
- Canned Fruits
- Rice
- Beans and Legumes – all kinds
- Beef/Chicken Broth and/or bullion
- Canned Meats
- Dried Mashed Potatoes (flakes)
- Dehydrated and Canned Vegetables
- Peanut Butter
- Oats / Oatmeal or rolled oats
- Raisins and other dried fruit
- Nuts, different kinds
- Spices; multiple small bottles
- Juice, can or bottle

The extended list has some cooking and baking essentials. As stated before, write down what your family consumes and let this list be a guide.

A rice and beans meal has the basic life sustaining amount of carbohydrates, protein and fat. It is the 'go-to' meal. But by eating rice and beans at every meal, one would become bored and appetite fatigue will result. Your mind and your body will simply reject the thought of eating the same food again and again and again.

Appetite fatigue does *not* occur when there is no food available but when there is food to eat and you choose to *not* eat. This is one of the reasons old people in a retirement home whose cafeteria serves the same basic bland food over and over again usually lose weight and therefore, their health. It would be the same with any survival food. The food supply *must* have a variety of food. Change up the menu by adding rice, barley, potato flakes or browned flour (Rue) to a soup or meal; this can stretch the servings and add needed nutrients.

The average American diet is loaded with sugar. This is neither advisable nor healthy. Some of the food on the list can be changed to make for a healthier choice but this *does* change up the shelf life. Check to see the shelf life on each new item.

All canned foods have a basic shelf life of one to five years but this is a manufacturer 'best by' date.
Beyond this date the color, taste and nutritional value start to fade, however the product is still edible.

A well believed myth is if there is no food, carrying extra weight or fat means you will last longer than a thin person. This is not true. You can still die from starvation and malnutrition being overweight to obese. Fat cells are stored energy, not stored nutrients.

Once a disaster/emergency hits you may choose to ration the food; making portions smaller or completely skipping a meal. This will help your supply last longer. Fasting for a day will not hurt you physically if you are healthy and fit. Adults can take turns skipping meals alternately or together to make it easier. Children younger than 16 years old should not fast or skip meals on purpose. Remember no matter how the food is rationed, you still need to drink plenty of water/fluid.

Three-Month Food Supply List
For a Family of Four or One Person for One Year

This list can be used for one adult one year's supply of food or rationed to fit the number of people in your family. Break up the list in half or fourths for the three and six month amount of time. Add items or substitute any item that you feel would work best for your family.

Quantity	Item
50 Pounds	Long Grain White Rice
50 Pounds	Whole Wheat Berries or Flour
30 Pounds	5 lb. Bag Corn Meal
4 Boxes	32 oz Buttermilk Complete Pancake Mix
4 Boxes	42 oz. Box Quaker Quick 1 Minute Oats
4 Boxes	5 lb. Box Quaker Quick Grits
36 Boxes	16 oz. Box Spaghetti Noodles
24 Cans	15 oz. Macaroni and Cheese

24 Cans	15 oz. Chef Boyardee ravioli, spaghetti
24 Cans	18.8 oz. Campbell's Chunky Soup
48 Cans	5 oz. Bumble Bee Tuna in Oil or Water
12 Cans	16 oz. Canned Ham
24 Cans	12 oz. Spam
24 Cans	5 oz. Vienna sausage
24 Cans	12 oz. Roast Beef
24 Cans	15 oz. Hormel Roast Beef/Corned Hash
48 Cans	14 oz. Can Beef Stew
48 Cans	15 oz. Chili with Beans/without beans
96 Cans	15 oz. Can Beans - different varieties
180 Cans	15 oz. Can Mixed Vegetables
12 Boxes	32 oz. Box Instant Potatoes
48 Cans	15 oz. Can Fruit Cocktail or sep. fruit
24 Cans	16 oz. Can Tomato Paste
12 Cans	4 oz. Can Sliced Mushrooms
12 Cans	10.75 oz. Can Cream of Chicken Soup
12 Boxes	64 oz. Box Powdered Instant Dry Milk
24 Cans	2 oz. Can Evaporated Milk
3 Boxes	32 oz. Box Velveeta Brand Cheese
12 Boxes	1 lb. Box Butter (or powder equivalent)
5 Jars	50.7 oz. Jar Extra-Virgin Olive Oil
2 Cans	3 lb. Can Crisco Shortening
12 Cans	8 oz. Hershey's Cocoa Powder
8 Cans	16 oz. Can Hershey's Cocoa Syrup
25 Pounds	5 lb. Bag White Granulated Sugar
6-12 Pounds	1 lb. Box Brown Sugar
6-12 Pounds	1 lb. Box Confection Sugar
12 Boxes	20 oz. Box Brownie Mix or Cake Mix
4 Jars	16 oz. Jar Light Corn Syrup
6 Jars	12.5 oz. Jar 100% Pure Maple Syrup
6 Jars	16 oz. Jar Clover Honey
12 Jars	18 oz. Jar Peanut Butter
12 Jars	16 oz. Jar Jelly or Preserves
48 Each	Beef Bouillon Large Cubes
48 Each	Chicken Bouillon Large Cubes
12 Boxes	16 oz. Box Corn Starch
24 Boxes	6 oz. Box Baking Soda

12 Jars	2.62 oz. Cream of Tartar
24 Pkgs	5/16 oz. Package Yeast - freeze
6 Bottles	2 oz. Bottle Vanilla Extract
24 Pounds	4 lb. Box Pure Salt Canning Pickling
12 Jars	2.6 oz. Ground Black Pepper
12 Jars	5.5 oz. Seasoned Meat Tenderizer
12 Jars	3.12 oz. Onion Powder
2 Jars	0.9 oz. Oregano
2 Jars	2.5 oz. Garlic Powder or Garlic Salt
2 Jars	2.37 oz. Cinnamon
1 Jar	1.75 oz. Cayenne Red Pepper
2 Bottles	15 oz. Bottle Lemon Juice
1 Gallon	Jug Apple Cider Vinegar in **glass** jar

As of the beginning of 2013, the cost of this food supply is roughly $1,775. This priced depends on where you shop, sales and discounted items. Each year the overall price has steadily gone up on most items. The prices will spike during a shortage.

Non-food items

For the toilet paper the amount is one roll per person per week. A family of four would go through four rolls a week; plus or minus depending on personal habits. Figure how much an item is used during a month's time then multiply it by twelve. That should give you an estimated amount to purchase.

Depending on the amount of storage room you have and what type of emergency/disaster and budget will all play into the total amounts of each non-food item you wish to purchase. For example, if you have a readily available water source, then buying paper plates for the convenience of not washing plates would be a waste of resources and create extra debris.

Paper Products
Toilet Paper (One roll per week per person)
Paper Towels
Feminine Products
Diapers/Wet Wipes – extras for clean up
Tissue
Paper Plates
Plastic Utensils
Napkins

Personal   Hygiene
Shampoo
Conditioner
Toothpaste
Toothbrushes
Deodorant
Antiperspirant
Face wash
Body wash/Soap
Shaving cream/razors
Aftershave
Lotion
Sponges - each person has their own different color

Cleaning Products
Laundry Detergent
Dishwashing soap
Bleach
All-Purpose Cleaner
Scrub brush

Miscellaneous Items
Light Bulbs
Candles/Kerosene Lamps
Lamp oil
Needles/Thread

Board Games/Cards
Books
Matches and lighters
Batteries of all sizes
Hand Sanitizers
Surgical Face Masks
Mace or Pepper spray
Dog/Cat Food
Extra Water for Pets
Kitty Litter
Heavy duty Work Glove

Continue your list here

Chapter Four

Emergency While Away from Home

An Emergency Kit is a tub, bag or box with a three day supply of food and survival essentials. Some call it BOB (bug out bag), GOOD bag (get-out-of-dodge bag), SHTF bag (*#%@ Hits the Fan bag) or the 72 hour bag, whatever the name, the bags are usually ready and easily obtained in case a quick get-away is needed. It is a *very* good idea to have the bag already assembled in the event of a short term evacuation scenario. When it is time to load up the car, most of the supplies are ready, just grab and go.

As the seasons change, make sure your car, truck or SUV is ready for anything. You may need snow tires, new windshield wipers and fluid, anti-freeze, heater/air conditioner service, recommended scheduled tune-ups, etc. When preparing your car for the possible unforeseen events, it is wise to make preparations for the driver and passengers as well.

When a disaster happens -- it might not be at the convenient time.

> *"A pessimist sees the difficulty in every opportunity; an optimist sees the opportunity in every difficulty."*
> *- Winston Churchill*

The Emergency Car Kit is crucial for breakdowns and unusual weather conditions. If the event leaves your automobile intact but the roads are filled with debris, for instance, an earthquake in California hits and the roads and bridges are cracked, you will not be able to drive home, so walking is your only option.

The emergency can be the car having mechanical problems or a disaster happening while you are on vacation or just a short distance from home. Either way, your first priority is to get to safety. Keep essential supplies in your car in case you get stranded for a few hours or even a few days.

Depending on how far away you are from home will determine the stopping points and safe spots. Start your trek home as soon as you can, although a friend or relatives home may be closer. Think things through before you start walking. A major disaster situation may mean *not* being able to go home at all. The only supply you have is in the kit. When the emergency hits -- the Emergency Car Kit is sitting in your car ready and waiting to go when you are.

Also if you are at home or on a road trip and an evacuation of the area is ordered, the Emergency Car Kit will be used first in route to safety. That supply being in the car, prior to packing for the evacuation frees one from the panic if there is not enough time to get everything done.

What should be kept in the Emergency Car Kit? First, you want to make sure you have the basic essentials such as water, food, and warmth. After these basics, you can add other necessities such as a flashlight, first aid kit, tools and other accessories.

Emergency Car Kit List

Place everything in a backpack, which is by far the most convenient way to carry everything in the event you have to leave your car.

Water:
Drinkable water is of utmost importance. Most people can actually survive days without food, but your body will dehydrate without water, leading to organ failure and death.

Water is also useful for washing wounds and for sanitation. Water can also be helpful if your car overheats. Because of the limited space in automobiles, storing water must be in small packages. Water is available in small drink boxes, in pouches or different size bottles. Different flavored packets (tang, crystal light, etc.) included in your kit can add variety and nutrition.

Food:
It is very difficult to keep food from spoiling in your car because it is exposed to extreme temperatures, both hot and cold. The best thing to store in your car is high energy bars. These bars come in packages of 2400 calories and 3600 calories. They are designed to handle extreme temperatures. They have tasty flavors, help you feel full and won't leave you thirsty.

You can purchase these types of bars online or at a camping supply store. Pack sealed nuts, granola, candy and anything else you want that does not melt or perish. Make sure you have enough for everyone in the car for at least three days. Better to have too much than not enough.

Warmth:

You may have plenty of food and water, but if you're cold you'll feel miserable. Especially in the winter, warmth is a must for an emergency car kit. There are several options

- 6 to 20 hour warm packs - warm packs are nice for quick, concentrated heat. You can put them in your pockets, shoes and gloves to stay warm.
- Wool blankets -wool is one of nature's warmest fibers. It provides warmth even when it's wet. It is best to get a wool blend blanket with synthetic fibers. They provide softness, wash-ability and durability.
- Emergency Blanket or Bag – reflects 80% to 90% of radiant body heat
- Poncho - for outside in the rain or other bad weather

Light:

It's important to always keep a flashlight in your emergency car kit. It comes in handy for all types of circumstances. Be sure to keep charged batteries in the flashlight so you aren't left in the dark. The Innovative LED Lights have a much higher battery life than conventional flashlights and are essential for emergency car kits.

Other forms are lightsticks and emergency candles with a wide base. Lightsticks last for 12 hours and are safe for children. They are visible up to one mile away, and they are non-toxic and non-flammable. Emergency candles or liquid paraffin candles are long-lasting, reusable, odorless and smokeless. A wide base adds stability, which helps prevent accidental spills. Also, be sure to keep lighters and waterproof matches in your emergency car kit.

First Aid Items:

A *basic* first aid kit allows you to aid people with minor injuries. To create a more comprehensive first aid kit add items such as

- Pain relievers
- Gauze pads
- Sterile pads
- Alcohol prep pads
- Antibacterial hand sanitizer
- Micro-pore tape
- Ace bandages
- Finger splint
- Ointment
- Assorted medications

Basic Tool Kit:

Purchase a small basic tool kit for quick fixes. The tool kit can stay separate from the backpack. Add to the kit tools such as

- A multi-purpose knife
- A collapsible shovel for your car (A shovel may come in handy if you are stuck in the snow or mud and for digging cat-holes)
- Crow bar OR Samurai survival tool provides an axe, hammer, and pry tool all-in-one.
- A roll of duct tape
- Work gloves
- Poncho – one size fits all type
- Tarp
- Rope - The rope and tarp can be used for a makeshift tent.
- Don't forget to pack a map

- Road flares. Flares should only be used for a warning signal, and should *never* be used for light. Make sure you set it on a non-flammable surface; the by-product from its fire drips to the ground and may cause a fire if it lands on flammable material such as grass or if there is a gas leak. Fumes are extremely nauseous and should be used in a well ventilated area.

Collect and place all the items in front of you, including the backpack. Make sure the items are the smaller, compact size, since you may have to carry these for an unknown distance. A heavier weight will take its toll on you. Pack everything you want. When time comes, you may decide to leave some of the heavier items behind.

Pack your backpack starting with the bigger items, placing the smaller items into side pockets and in between. The Kit can now be placed in the trunk or behind a seat. If you know the weather is going to reach extreme temperatures, remove the backpack for the day and/or night and return the pack the next time you go to the car.

The pack is very practical when going out for the day or on a hike. Place extra water in your car. You may find you need water for other reasons besides drinking. For examples, the car may overheat, for washing hands or rinsing dirty feet before getting into the car.

Remember to replenish anything you take out of your car kit as soon as possible.

Babies and Toddlers Kit

A comprehensive list of things you may want to consider including in your Emergency Car Kit if you ever have babies or toddlers in the car at *any* time. Remember these are only guidelines,

- **Instant formula -** Make sure it is the kind you need to mix with water. The extreme temperatures will not affect powder
- **4 small bottles for the formula -** You can fill them with purified water to provide extra drinking water in your kit if you do not need them
- **Plenty of diapers -** The exact number depends on the age of your child. Also 3 cloth ones that can be washed, dried and reused
- **A travel package of wipes -** These are great for washing. If there is space, store a full size box of wet wipes
- **Pacifiers -** Just in case
- **Baby food -** Depending on the age of your child you will probably want to include some jars of baby food
- **Small comfort toy/s -** If you child has a specific toy or blanket that he/she really loves, try to grab that in an emergency
- **Clothes – and plenty of them!** Babies grow fast so replace the clothes in the car kit when you switch the clothes in the closet. Include clothes for all types of weather and include lots of spares
- **Ziploc bags -** These work great for used diapers or anything else that is dirty
- **Infant Tylenol/Motrin -** Keep this item with the rest of the first aid kit

- **Desatin or other diaper rash cream and travel-sized baby powder** - This will be useful if you have to resort to using cloth diapers

Continue your list here

Chapter Five

Prep for a Long Term Event

What if a short term event goes long term? The answer is completely relative. What is a short amount of time? If you have a two week supply - then any time less than that is considered short term. You are set and are able to live somewhat normal during the emergency. A blizzard that keeps you at home with plenty of food, water and games to play by candle light while you sip hot cocoa doesn't seem so horrible.

But ... the opposite is also true. If you have a two week supply and the emergency/disaster lasts three weeks then the last week will be really tough. If you run out of water, you will not last long and will have to seek a new water source. Your survival will depend partially on the resources available *before* the situation developed and also your ability to find and create a continuous food supply after your supply has been exhausted.

"A prudent man foresees the difficulties ahead and prepares for them; the simpleton goes blindly on and suffers the consequences."
- Proverbs 22:3 (NLT)

Stay or Go?

There may come a time when a disaster makes the home unlivable, i.e. wildfire and /or smoke, earthquake, flood, gas leak, etc. and evacuating is necessary. Survival books, web sites and guides urge the masses to have a retreat location to store up your food, guns and ammo. Most people do not have the income and/or resources to buy a retreat cabin in the woods. Let alone the time to dedicate to filling the cabin with all the survival supplies needed.

If your family consensus is to bug out right away, you will need to plan on the where... and when... and how you are going to get there. Everything comes down to where you live and what you are willing to do. In any case, research and planning is essential for every kind of scenario before it happens.

The number one question that should be decided on is...
If the emergency last longer than _____ amount of time, we will go. And if we go, we will go_____ (where?).

Your choices are ... staying at home, evacuating to a shelter or...you can evacuate and live with a friend or relative or... disappear into the *wilderness*.

If a disaster happened right now, how would your family react? One way to find out how your family would react is to play the "Oh no, the electricity is out" game... Go shut off the electricity when no one knows it's going to happen. See if you could cook a meal, wash dishes, etc. If you want to make a big impression – shut off the water, too. No using the toilet -- that will agitate a few people.

You will be surprised at how many times you flip a light switch and say 'oh that's right – no electricity', or turn the faucet on expecting water but get none. Do this for a few hours and you will feel both panic and a sense of peace when you know all you have to do is flip the switch and it will all go back to normal. This will not be so when a disaster happens.

Now, after doing this little test, did you see any holes in your preparations? Does everyone know where a flashlight is located? Do you have the 'do not open the refrigerator or freezer' rule established? Can your supply of batteries last a few weeks of everyday use? Do you have enough wood and/or propane for cooking? Feeling a bit unprepared?

This test will steel your resolve.

When it is Time to Go

If you have to evacuate your house, you may have as little as 10 minutes. Your town or city will inform you when it is time to go. But at the first sign of problems it might be best to bug out at your own convenience.

Under the stress of the circumstances, trying to think of what to save and what to leave can be very difficult. Take some time now to think about what items you will take with you. Write down a list of the high priority items you would take if you only had 10 minutes to evacuate your house. If you have time you can expand your packing from the priority "A" list to include your "B" list as well. Remember, you *may* have to carry everything.

A natural disaster destroys personal property but when the time comes, life returns to 'normal' and you may return to your home, be prepared it may have been scavenged through and picked clean. Add to that, human destructive tendencies and windows and doors may be broken. Getting life back to normal is a topic that is multifaceted. Location, townships infrastructure and personal readiness will make or break a family's ability to cope with the job of getting back on ones feet.

Stay at Home

This is easily the best way to ride out a short or long term event that does not make the house unlivable. If you live in an area that is conducive to staying home then a supply can be kept at the house. The only way that this would *not* work is if the emergency or disaster was very local and the house or neighborhood is in direct danger as with a wildfire, chemical spill, are downwind of a nuclear blast or in the danger zone from a nuclear plant melt down.

You may also find yourself having to leave the area *if* your short terms supplies get used up and there is no long term water supply. The key to staying at home 'long term' is a water source, heat, security and food source (garden and/or farm animals).

You can also continue to stock up on your supplies and barter items creating a long term supply. Skills are also great for bartering. Find neighbors, family and/or friends that you can make into a core 'Survival Group'. If you live in a suitable location, other people might need to come to your house in the case of their evacuation.

If this is likely to happen then a meeting to set up a plan with boundaries and perimeters of behavior needs to be discussed and agreed upon in advance of the emergency.

Evacuate to a Shelter

Find out where the evacuation shelter is located for your area. Most public schools will be quickly turned into a makeshift shelter if they are not affected by the disaster. This will allow the Government agencies and Red Cross and to deliver some needed supplies. But realize that if the event covers a large area, people who are not prepared and rely on the government to take care of them will be there in full force and herded like cattle. You may not be able to leave once you are there.

If you own pets, they will not be allowed inside the public shelter. You will need to make other provisions for your pets care prior to arriving at the shelter. Or leave them to fend for themselves; which is not recommended if they are domesticated and not used to taking care of themselves. You will sleep right next to people you do not know and even be accosted with germs and bacteria from living in close quarters. Al in all, it is up to you if this is the way you wish to go. But, in my opinion, a public shelter should be a last ditch option and only if *all* other options are not feasible.

Evacuate to a Friend or Relative's Home

If you decide to go to a friend or relative's home, all rules should be set up in advance.

The old saying about how familiarity breeds contempt could very well be true if steps are not taken to facilitate a smooth and working relationship.

Once the rules and boundaries are set up then it may be best to store your supplies there. If that is not possible, then renting a storage place that is open 24 hours a day, and is close enough that you can get there by walking -- if it were to come to that -- is the next best kind of storage and retreat plan.

Wilderness

If you chose the wilderness as your location after an emergency/disaster, then prepare yourself for a very long camping trip. Scout areas ahead of time. This choice is not for the weak-of-heart.

See if you can find a location with all the amenities of a fresh water stream within walking distance, flat land to garden and be strategically placed midway on a hill not too exposed to the elements and outcroppings to hide and hunt. The wilderness is only half the battle.

In a worst case scenario, the world is in total chaos, there is fallout or total collapse of civilization and life as we know it is no more, if you chose to live in the wilderness, then you must be ready to live like a rabbit or small animal that is considered prey. You may be able to forage for food, find plenty of firewood and build a sturdy campsite, but you must also be hidden enough so the human scavengers will not bother you. This 'hiding from the unknown' way of life is very non-aggressive. All people are not bad but it is better to be very cautious of anyone you come in contact with then to be caught unaware.

Preparing an Evacuation Plan

An emergency evacuation plan has two parts: evacuation from your house and evacuation from your neighborhood or town. An evacuation plan from your home is useful not only for major disasters, but also for smaller events like fires, gas leak or other incidents in your home. In some cases, an event will come with some warning and you will have time to pack and bug out. If an evacuation is ordered, *those who are prepared* will have a jump on all the others. The unprepared will be stuck in heavy traffic. Your bug out bags will be ready, food easily transported to the truck/car, clothes already chosen and ready to be thrown into a large tote. Your emergency list will be available and items easily obtained. *You are already in the car and on the road* when most are thinking of what they might need to put into a suitcase - which is stored somewhere in the basement or garage.

A general list of evacuation items is in the back of the book. Please spend some time thinking about what is on the list; add or take out whatever you feel is necessary. This is *your* plan. Important points to remember when creating an evacuation plan are:

- Have at least two (2) escape routes from each room. Usually a door and window
- Locations of any escape ladders, or other special equipment.
- Locations of fire extinguishers, first aid kits, 72 hour kit.
- Locations of the shutoffs for gas, water, and electricity
- Who gets who? – small children and animals
- Know the closest evacuation centers

- Determine meeting spots outside the affected area
- Main and alternative routes for leaving the city in North, South, East and West directions.

Give some thought to what things you need to do to secure your house. Write down your plans and keep the paper in a safe and accessible location. Be sure that each family member has a copy of the evacuation plan, maps and telephone numbers.

Place to Meet:
At the time of an emergency, your family may not be together. Remember that bridges may be out and roads may be blocked by debris, so choose your meeting places carefully with access in mind. Pick places that are easy to identify, that can be reached on foot if necessary, and that is within an accessible open area. Take into account where each of you will likely be at different times and on different days. By plotting out potential routes on a city map before the disaster, you will save yourself from having to figure something out while in a hurry.

Choose an Out-of-Area Contact:
During an emergency local phone service may be limited, so you should arrange with someone outside your area to be your family contact. Your contact person should have voice mail or an answering machine. Ensure that every family member knows to listen to the radio or TV for telephone use instructions, then phone the out-of-area contact person to let them know how and where they are located and what their plans are.

Things to think about when crafting your area evacuation plan include: routes to avoid, obvious hazards, or routes which are likely to be impassable in a disaster (old bridges that could collapse). You probably will want to drive the routes before deciding and avoid common routes that may be congested during an emergency.

Each family member should carry a list of the 3 contacts. In an emergency each person can contact the persons out of the emergency area to pass along messages and check on the welfare of other family members. Keep calls short to keep lines clear for others, and if possible, arrange to call back at a specified time for another check-in.

You may also want to inquire about emergency plans at places where your family spends most of their time: work, daycare and school. If no plans exist, consider volunteering to help create one.

Talk to your neighbors about how you can work together in the event of an emergency. You will be better prepared to reunite with your family if you plan ahead and communicate with others in advance.

Timed Evacuation

The time to evacuate is usually when the government tells a large area of an impending disaster. But sometimes (such as an earthquake) there is no 'heads-up' or a defined time to leave.

This is where your survival group has to come up with a definitive event and time frame to evacuate your homes and head for the designated location.

The amount of time to grab what is needed, lock down everything and get out of the house should take the least amount of time possible. The more you have prepared the house for lock down along with a packed and ready bug out bag, the easier it will be to get out *fast*.

Test yourself to see if you can pull off total evacuation and shutting down the house within 5 to 10 minutes. This includes shutting off gas and water and locking all windows and doors. Skip the actual gas shutoff, since it might need to be turned back on by a professional. Just know where the shut off is located.

If you tried the test run and were able to gather your needed supply and lock up within the 5 minutes then you did very well. But if you are like most people then a portion of your important items were sprawled all over the house. It most likely took more than 15 minutes for an individual and 10 minutes for a family to gather everything. If everything is in an easily accessible place the collecting time will be cut in half. This is why an Evacuation List and Emergency Binder are essential.

After an ordered evacuation has been established, the majority of people will take the total amount of allowed time to gather up personal items. But after you have gathered items for your evacuation bag, practiced the test run and lock down, you will be one of the first on the road and *way* ahead of everyone else. The others will be met with loads of traffic, gas lines and shortages.

The Family Evacuation Grab List

The Evacuation Grab List will be in the back of the book. This way the book can be bent back and the page made visible, making the list easier to read and follow.

The space provided is for your ideas and thoughts

"The only mistake in life is the lesson not learned,"
                                    -- Albert Einstein

Chapter Six

Food Storage and Preserving

After you have your emergency/disaster car and 72 hour kits taken care of and in place, your focus should now be on the longer term food storage. With a bit of planning, your food storage will have what you need to *make* actual meals. Knowing what you need is essential - you don't want to end up with a year's supply of wheat and be unable to make a loaf of bread because you do not have any of the other ingredients. Anything you might need to run to the store to get -- is right there in your storage supply.

Consider your storage area your personal mini-mart grocery store.

The difference is -- since this is *your* store, the supplies are replenished by you. The foods you have on the shelves cannot be replenished during a disaster or emergency. Meaning, you have to learn how to jar, pickle, dry, cook and bake to sustain the family's food cupboard and pantry after the disaster.

"In the house of the wise are stores of choice food and oil, but a foolish man devours all he has."
Proverbs 21:20 *(NIV)*

Shelf Life

The food storage consist of jar and can food, such as fruit, meat and vegetables, as well as dried and dehydrated foods like pasta, rice, beans and legumes (lentils, split pea, etc.). Dried mixes, spices, sauces, gravies and bullions are also stored. All of these items are best if used by the "For Best Quality Use By" date found stamped on the top or bottom of cans. The coding will vary from manufacturer to manufacturer but usually includes when and where it was packaged.

For month coding, if a number is used, numbers 1 through 9 represent January through September, and letters O for October, N for November and D for December. If letters are used, A=Jan. and L=Dec., unless otherwise noted. For year coding; 8=1998; 9=1999; 0=2000; 1=2001; 2=2002, and so on, is used.

The general rule is that canned food has a shelf life of at least two years from the date of purchase if stored at normal temperatures of 75° or less. Commercial canning is a high-heat process that renders the food sterile; it retains safety and nutritional value well beyond two years; however some change in color and texture may take place. If the can has any signs of damage, botulism may be present. If the can is intact, not dented or bulging, it is edible. In fact, canned food has an almost indefinite shelf life; cans as old as 100 years have been found in sunken ships still microbiologically safe.

Grains and Cereal

Before you buy big, look into the shelf life of the food you wish to purchase. Some food containers are not meant to store the items for anything longer than a few days or weeks. Switch dried foods (beans, rice, pasta, etc.) to an air tight food grade container. These foods have a very long shelf life of 10 plus years *if* they are stored properly in a cool, dry place.

All flours are not the same. They each have specific uses and shelf life. Whole wheat flour becomes "enriched white flour" when the bran and germ are removed. To make up for the removal of nutrients, riboflavin, niacin, thiamine, vitamin A and iron are added back into the flour. Whole grain flour does not have its bran removed which contains a higher fat content and will then spoil faster.

Corn Flakes and Cheerios will hold out and stay fresh longer than other whole grain products. Like white flour, some cereals have had their fat-containing bran and germ removed, not the best choice for healthy digestion, but the cereal will do in an emergency. Ready-to-eat cereals will last one full year in unopened boxes stored in cool, dry places. This is a conservative time frame, especially if the cereal is stored in air tight containers.

Food storage sites and stores sell the large pails of hard red or hard white wheat (berries). There are many kinds of whole grains available which include barley, buckwheat, hominy (cracked corn), millet, oats, rye, rice and wheat. The large storage pails can be opened with a pail opener or wrench. Take what you need and close it back up again. You can then grind it into flour or cook it whole or placed into a sprout grower. (See How to grow sprouts)

Once the pail is opened air has been introduced, the contents need to be consumed within a shorter time than the 10 year shelf life -- unless the air is again removed by using an oxygen absorber available at emergency essentials and supply websites.

White rice can last indefinitely as does pasta with proper storage. White rice has its bran removed, allowing it to last longer than brown rice. Sometimes in order to make up for the loss of vitamins and minerals, nutrients are added back in. Wild rice, which is not even rice but a grass seed, lasts as long as white rice.

There is a large amount of produce that is not commonly mass production. The common ones like wheat, corn, oat and barley are only four out of hundreds of edible grains. There are over 500 different kinds of potato, beans and legumes, but we only see about 15 different kinds in the grocery store. So, change it up and explore new possibilities. This is where the fun of learning and prepping can be seen and shared.

Other Types of Foods
Herbs and spices, when dried are long-lasting. You can grow them yourself then dry them for use later or use fresh in your cooking.

Sugar, sugar substitutes, honey and salt when properly stored last forever. Molasses, maple syrup and hard candy will last for years if placed in an airtight container. Salt can be useful in preserving fish and other meats. Sugary foods may be considered luxuries, but "comfort foods" will help stabilize moods in uneasy times. Coffee, ground or instant, will last one full year if the container is not opened or sealed. This seems conservative but the oils can go rancid and affect the taste. Tea can last between 6-12 months. But as Tea is dried, it should last, as long as humidity does not get to it.

Dried milk powder will last 10 years or longer if well cared for. Reconstituted dried milk is better used for baking than as a beverage. Have a supply of powdered butter and powdered cheese to be used as a substitute in recipes that ask for fresh but fresh is not available.

MRE – Meals Ready to Eat

While growing your own fruits and vegetables makes very good economical and survivaling sense, pre-packaged meals ready to eat (MRE) are a great survivalist staple. The temperature the MRE is stored will dictate how long the MRE will last. If you wish to leave a small supply in your car where the temperatures are wildly fluctuating between extreme hot and freezing the MRE will last only a few months. But, if a box of MRE's is placed somewhere cool, with little to no fluctuating temperature, they will last up to 130 months.

Usually the MRE's are eaten first as a convenient emergency food since they are very high in calories and energy. Most military personnel have found that eating only MRE for a few days will bind up their intestines causing discomfort. Therefore, it is wise to ration MRE's and change up the types of food consumed.

MRE's can be bought at most places where dry and dehydrated foods for camping, hiking or survival type items are sold. Some MRE's are tasty and then some others are totally disgusting. Eat a few to see which ones your family likes, then store that kind of MRE for up to 25 years. Have a selection of MRE's, dehydrated foods along with a variety of dried foods can make the short term emergency or disaster more bearable...or they can last for years while waiting patiently for the emergency to happen. Either way they are convenient, expensive, but convenient.

Animals
Depending on the situation, keeping animals might be a possibility. Other survivalists suggest having *no* livestock or pets because they can draw attention to you when being invisible may be the best choice, while still others insist on keeping every kind of animal. This decision is completely up to the individual. If you have the land, you may choose to keep goats instead of cows, since cows take up more area and eat more. Keeping chickens comes with the obvious benefits of fresh eggs and meat and might be the right choice for you. Goats will give milk and provide meat, as will chickens, ducks, geese and rabbits. As for the horse, dog and cat; they work for their keep.

Preserving Fresh Fruit and Vegetables

Food storage methods have been used for centuries; long before electricity was harnessed. Each method has unique benefits. For now, we have the ability to use all of them. The basic preserving methods can be used together or separately. These will sustain you while your garden is in the off season. Come summer and fall harvest, you can replenish your supply for the next winter. Use any and all types of preserving to widen your food storage options. The basic types that can be used are:
• Freeze
• Refrigeration
• Root Cellar

- Dehydration / Drying
- Salt and Brine
- Smoking Meat
- Vacuum Food Sealer
- Lacto-Fermentation
- Water Bath Canning
- Steam Pressure Canning

Freeze

Fresh produce contains chemical compounds called enzymes which cause flavor changes and the loss of color and nutrients in frozen fruits and vegetables. These enzymes become active once the produce is harvested, they must be un-activated to prevent such reactions from taking place.

Enzymes in vegetables are inactivated by the blanching process. In most cases, blanching is absolutely essential for producing quality frozen vegetables. Blanching is the exposure of the vegetables to boiling water or steam for a brief period of time. The vegetable must then be rapidly cooled in ice water to prevent it from cooking.
Blanching also helps to destroy microorganisms on the surface of the vegetable and to make some vegetables, such as broccoli and spinach, more compact.

Some vegetables like lettuce and celery along with whole tomatoes should not be frozen due to the high water content in the cells. The freezing process destroys many of the cell walls which then make it mushy when defrosted. The amount of cell wall rupture can be controlled by freezing produce as quickly as possible.

Rapid freezing causes a large number of small ice crystals to be formed producing less cell wall rupture than slow freezing which produces only a few large ice crystals. Textural changes due to freezing are not as noticeable in foods that are cooked before eating because cooking also softens cell walls. These changes are also less noticeable in high starch vegetables, such as peas and corn.

The breakdown of enzymes in fruit is what causes the discoloration and loss of vitamin C. Because fruits are usually served raw, they are not blanched like vegetables. Instead, enzymes in frozen fruit are controlled by using chemical compounds which stop or slow down the chemical reaction. The most common form is ascorbic acid. One can also try soaking the fruit in dilute vinegar solutions or coating the fruit with sugar and lemon juice. However, these do not prevent browning as effectively as using ascorbic acid. Overloading the freezer with unfrozen products will result in a long, slow freeze and a poor quality product. Before putting a large amount of unfrozen items inside the freezer, turn it to the lowest setting. Some fruits, vegetables, meats and grains can and should be stored in other ways for the best quality.

Root Cellar

The root cellar (or cold cellar) was an essential part of every home in the days before fresh produce was available in supermarkets. Year-round underground cellars keep a steady temperature of 40°- 60° during winter's freeze or summer's heat. The food was kept there for easy retrieval and the root cellar is again starting to gain popularity in the main stream population.

Root crops, winter squash and some other homegrown items like jams, jelly, bread, salted meat, butter, cheese and even milk and cream can be kept in a root cellar. This will not keep them from spoiling but will prolong their life for a short time more. If the fruit or vegetable is kept cool, it will last for months. If the jams and jellies are canned, then they can last for years.

There are certain fruits and vegetable that will not do well and will rot. It is important to harvest vegetables at their peak for best longevity while in storage. The slightest bruising invites mold and bacteria, then it will spread to other vegetables. As soon as you see a rotting or molding vegetable, get rid of it. Slice off the bad part and eat the rest, or throw it into the compost heap. Get into the habit of inspecting cellar foods often.

The following list is how long certain vegetables can keep in the root cellar and the ideal temperatures and humidity for each item. If you cannot have multiple cellars or temperature controlled areas, the shelf placement is the next best way to will help stretch the life of each fruit or vegetable. Root cellar products that are best stored in cold and very moist conditions (35°- 40°F and 90-95% relative humidity). These should be stored toward the bottom shelves where there is more moisture:

- Beets 4-5 mo
- Broccoli 1-2 wks
- Brussels sprouts 3-5 wks
- Carrots 4-6 mo
- Celery – 6+mo
- Chinese cabbage 1-2 mo
- Collards 1-2 wks
- Jerusalem artichokes 1-2 mo
- Kohlrabi – 6+ mo
- Leeks
- Parsley
- Parsnips 1-2 mo
- Radishes 2-3 mo
- Rutabagas 2-4 mo
- Turnips 6+

The following produce do very well in the same cool temperature but slightly less humidity (80-90%): These should be stored in the middle shelves.

- Apples 3-6 mo
- Cabbage – 6+ mo
- Cauliflower 2-4 wks
- Endive
- Escarole
- Grapefruit
- Grapes
- Oranges
- Pears
- Potatoes 4-6 mo
- Quince
- Cantaloupe 1-2 wks
- Cucumbers 2-3 wks
- Eggplant 1-2 wks
- Sweet peppers 2-4 mo
- Tomatoes 1-2 mo
- Watermelon 1-2 wks

The following need higher temperatures and lower humidity (50°- 60° and 60-70% humidity). Placed on the very top shelf:

- Hot peppers 2-3 wks
- Pumpkins 2-4 mo
- Sweet potatoes 6+ mo
- Winter squash 4-6 mo

Reduce the temperature and humidity of the following vegetables (35°- 45° and 60-70% humidity): These are better if dried/dehydrated if wanting to extend their use.

- Garlic 1-2 mo
- Onions 1-2 mo

Remember that they will often remain edible longer than the times given. Although every case will not be exactly the same, use this list as a guide for determining how long the produce will last and plant your garden accordingly. You may want to plant lots of potatoes and carrots as they will last 4-6 months in the cellar, while you would not plant a lot of broccoli since it will only keep for a few weeks. Leafy vegetables are not included as they generally will not keep well in a root cellar but you can preserve them in other ways.

Some produce will not last long if they are kept in the refrigerator, for instance, carrots, even when wrapped in plastic bags will only last 7-14 days. But if they become rubbery after a certain time, you can boil them in soup or preserve them as relishes in vinegar. In an emergency most can handle eating carrots in almost any state.

Dehydration and Drying

Dehydrating foods will free one from the concern about botulism, is low cost, require less storage space than canned goods and there's no freezer to keep running. If you have a surplus of fruits or vegetables from your garden, but lack the canning equipment or freezer space, drying may be the right method for you. Foods can be dried in a conventional oven, a commercial dehydrator, or in the sun. Drying times vary with the method and foods chosen. Dehydration of lean cuts of meat can be done in any of the fore mentioned methods. (See "How to make Jerky")

Preparation
- Select the best fruits and vegetables - choose ones that are ripe, unblemished and at their peak

- Prepare the food as you want them to be served -Apples, for example, may be sliced, cut into rings, or pureed for fruit leather (dry puree to resemble leather then roll off plastic wrap)
- Keep the meat all the same size and thickness for even drying time
- Foods left intact need to be washed - herbs, berries and seedless grapes
- To prevent browning, try steaming or coating fruits and vegetables with acids such as lemon juice or ascorbic acid (Fruit Fresh) before drying
- Steaming or blanching is necessary for vegetables to inactivate the enzymes that cause vegetables to mature, or toughen during drying
- If you are drying in the sun, make sure it is away from insects, try placing the tray inside close to a sunny window

During Drying

- Maintain 130°F to 140°F, with circulating air, this will help remove the moisture as quickly as possible to prevent spoilage without adversely affecting food's texture, color, flavor and nutritive value
- If the initial temperature is low, or air circulation is insufficient, foods may undergo undesirable microbiological changes before drying adequately
- If the temperature is too high, or humidity too low, nutrients can be lost
- When your food is dry it should be pliable and leathery and should contain about 10 percent moisture

After Drying (for fruit only)

- The moisture content of home dried fruit should be about 20 percent. When the fruit is taken from the dehydrator, the remaining moisture may not be distributed equally among the pieces because of their size or their location in the dehydrator. Conditioning is the process used to equalize the moisture content thus reducing the risk of mold growth

- To condition the fruit, take the dried fruit that has cooled and pack it loosely in plastic or glass jars. Seal the containers and let them stand for 7 to 10 days. The excess moisture in some pieces will be absorbed by the drier pieces

- Allow dried fruit (not vegetables) time to condition for 4 to 10 days before packaging for storage

- Shake the jars or bags daily to separate the pieces and check the moisture condensation

- If condensation develops in the jar, return the fruit to the dehydrator for more drying

Packaging and Storing

- Use tightly sealed containers, such as moisture-proof freezer containers or Ziploc type bags, or sanitized glass jars
- Pack as tightly as possible without crushing
- Pack food in amounts that will be used in a recipe; every time a package is re-opened, the food is exposed to air and moisture that will lower the quality of the food.

- Store the jars or bags in a cool, dark, dry place
- The higher the temperature the shorter the shelf life
- Most dried fruits can be stored for 1 year at 60°F, 6 months at 80°F
- Vegetables have about half the shelf-life of fruits
- For best quality, use foods within 6 to 12 months

Salt and Brine

Brine is a saltwater solution which is 1 cup of salt to one quart of pure water. This ratio is used to preserve meat by covering the meat completely. Packing meat in salt by itself also works to preserve it, just rinse the salt off before cooking.

Smoking Meat

To smoke meat you will need an enclosed fire pit. A couple of ponchos wrapped around three poles, set up like a tepee with smaller thin sticks tied from one to the other (for support), will house the smoke. Dig a pit to house the fire and keep a close eye on it. It does not need to be big since the intent is smoke, not heat. Use hardwoods for the best flavor. Green resinous wood will smoke but will ruin the taste of the meat.

Season the meat how you wish then cut it into thin slices, drape over the sticks without letting the meat touch. Keep the poncho closed to keep in the smoke. Meat smoked overnight will last about a week, smoked for two days will preserve the meat for two to four weeks. Properly smoked meat will look like a dark curled up stick and you can eat the jerky without further cooking.

Vacuum Food Sealer

Vacuum sealing will preserve the freshness and original flavor significantly which extends the shelf life approximately three to five times longer than if the food is not sealed. If you use vacuum sealed storage bags you will not need to use the oxygen absorber packets. The vacuum sealing process will remove all the oxygen from inside the specially designed bags.

Vacuum sealing is not a substitute for refrigeration or freezing. Any food item than needs to be refrigerated or frozen will still need to be kept in the refrigerator or freezer after you vacuum seal it; sealing will help that food item remain edible about 3 to 5 times longer than if it wasn't sealed. It will eliminate the problem with freezer burn because you will have isolated the food from the cold dry air inside the freezer.

Many foods can be protected from insects, oxygen, and humidity by sealing them inside a vacuum seal bag. Some examples of items you can vacuum seal are salt and peppercorns, baking items such as baking soda, corn starch, flour, sugar, corn meal, also dry noodles, grits and instant potatoes, oatmeal flakes, and instant milk among many others.

A good quality food vacuum sealer will cost around $40, and a two-roll box of vacuum seal bags will cost about $22. If you buy the 11-inch wide rolls that are 16-feet long, you can cut individuals bags from the roll to the exact length you need. This will allow you to seal a small item without using a large bag. You can also seal the foods in the quantities you will need; opening one bag at a time ensures the rest of your food will remain fresh inside its own vacuum sealed bag. Use a permanent marker to write the date and description of the contents.

Lacto-Fermentation

Before the advent of modern day canning most of our ancestors took fruit and vegetables and cultured them through a process called lacto fermentation. They had crocks of real sauerkraut and lacto-fermented cucumber pickles. Kim chi from Korea and Cortido from Latin America are two of the many flavorful concoctions not native to our own country. (See "How to Ferment, Lacto-, recipes' section in Chapter 9)

Traditionally, fermented vegetables were made simply with salt, water and spices. The lactic acid that was produced during the fermentation process would prevent the rotting of the vegetables which otherwise would not last through the winter in the root cellar.

Using this food preservation technique, unparalleled health benefits ensue. The fermentation of vegetables enhanced their digestibility and increases vitamin levels. Beneficial organisms are produced along with numerous helpful enzymes; acting as antibiotic and anti-carcinogenic substances. It also promotes the growth of healthy flora throughout the intestine. These microfloras (the good bacteria) make it hard for the bad bacteria to live and helps improve the immune system.

Sauerkraut is a great way to start on fermented vegetables. Pickled vegetable are possibly even easier than sauerkraut. There are different recipes to try and you can add or take away veggies that you wish. You may enjoy the process of trying new things from long ago.

All you need is: Wide mouth jar, something to weigh the veggies down below the water level, fresh vegetables, a knife or food processor, sea salt, spices, purified water and if you want, you may add whey to speed up the process. (See How to Make Whey in Chapter 8) The basic idea is to cover the vegetables with brine then time will allow the bacteria to do its thing.

Home Canning

Canning is an old method that helped to preserve the harvest to be consumed during the winter months. There are two different ways to can. The type of food you want to preserve will determine which method you will use; Water Bath or Steam Pressure.

The Water Bath Canners heat the water to 212°F, which removes the air to stop the natural spoilage from high-acid foods like tomatoes, salsa, jellies, jams, fruits, sauces, chutneys and pie filling.

In very high elevations the water begins to boil at a lower degree, somewhere near 185, thus creating a disadvantage in killing off the bacteria. A longer time on the heat source is then needed.

Recently, food scientists proved the risk of botulism poisoning from canned tomato products so acid is now added to commercially canned tomatoes. The higher acid levels will not allow bacteria to grow.

In foods such as meats, poultry, vegetables, chili, fish and other low acid foods, the Steam Pressure Home Canner is used. The much higher temperatures of 240°F, eliminates the risk of spoilage caused by the bacteria Clostridium botulium and its toxin-producing spores.

The simple instructions are found in canning recipe books. Each kind of food requires a *different* recipe for preparation, *different* fill levels in the jars and *different* amounts of time spent being processed.

The basic supply needed for the water-bath method is a 16 to 21-Quart Water-Bath Canner with canning rack or equally large Stockpot with a canning rack, jars with bands and lids along with common kitchen utensils: Sauce pan, Measuring spoons and cups, Cutting board, Kitchen knives, Ladle, Large spoon, Non-metallic spatula and dish rags

Jar prep
- Wash jars, lids and bands in hot, soapy water
- Rinse well
- Keep jars warm/hot until ready to use. You can keep them hot in a pot of simmering water. This will minimize the risk of breakage when filling with hot food
- Keep rack out until ready to use
- Fill the Water-Bath Canner half full or with enough water to cover the jars and heat to a simmer
- Place the cover on the canner

Select your recipe
Read the directions thoroughly. This is not the time to experiment with different amounts and ingredients, even the slightest change can ruin the taste and safety.
- Prepare your recipe
- Use the ladle to scoop the mixture into the hot jars Leaving the proper amount of headroom space between the rim and mixture
- Insert a knife or small spatula between the mixture and the side of the glass jar, removing any trapped bubbles

- Wipe off any drips
- Place the lid and band on the jar, finger tighten

Time

- Place the jars on the rack, when all jars are ready, lower the rack into the simmering water
- Make sure the water covers over the tops of the jars by at least an inch
- Return to boil, once the water boils – start the timer

Recipes are written for altitudes up to 1,000 feet above sea level. If needed, adjust the time for altitude.

Altitude Feet	Add to Processing Time
1,001 - 3,000	5 minutes
3,001 - 6,000	10 minutes
6,001 - 8,000	15 minutes
8,001 - 10,000	20 minutes

- Once the allotted time has passed, turn off heat and let jars stand in water for 5 minutes
- Remove jars from water and cool upright on wire rack or towel undisturbed for 12 hours
- Do not re-tighten bands that may have come loose during canning, this may interfere with the sealing process

When the 12 hours is up and jars are cool, press on center of lid. If jars have sealed properly, the lid will not flex up or down. You have successfully canned. If stored in a cool, dark place the jars can be stored for up to a year.

If the lid flexes, the jar has not sealed. Any jar that fails to seal can be reprocessed in a clean jar with a new lid or use it first within a few days.

Steam Pressure Canning

Steam Pressure canning has the same basic preserving recipes with instructions as the water-bath canner preparations. Each method has to be followed exactly to insure the integrity and safety of the food. Items you will need

- Pressure canner – follow the directions to the letter!
- All the items from the water-bath canning list (preserving jars, lids and bands, etc.) along with common kitchen utensils, such as wooden spoon, ladle and funnel
- Fresh vegetables, meat, poultry or seafood

Canning tips

- Add acid (lemon juice, vinegar or citric acid) to tomato products when directed in the recipe. Lemon juice is widely available, but will add a sharp note to canned tomatoes; citric acid will change the flavor less noticeably, and vinegar is part of many recipes anyway.
- If necessary, you can balance the tart taste by adding sugar
- Do know the Heating/Canning Process - water bath canning or pressure canning - as called for in each recipe
- Canning jars - Use standard mason jars for home canning. Commercial food jars that are not heat-tempered, such as mayonnaise jars often break
- Discard any with cracks, chips, dents or rust. Defects prevent airtight seals
- The flat lids can be used only once, but the screw bands can be reused as long as they are in good condition

- Do not use overripe fruit. If you start out with low quality, it will only get worse in storage
- Do not add more low-acid ingredients (onions, celery, peppers, garlic, etc.) than specified in the recipe. This may result in an unsafe product
- Do not add substantially more seasonings or spices - these items are often high in bacteria and excess spices can make a canned item unsafe
- Do not add butter or fat to home-canned products unless stated in a tested recipe - butters and fats do not store well and may increase the rate of spoilage
- Thickeners - with the exception of "Clear-Jell" which has been tested in USDA and university food labs, do not thicken with starches, flour, or add rice, barley or pasta to mixtures
- Always add boiling water when needed, keep water level one inch above the tops of the jars

Cooking Points

- When available, use shortening to grease baking pans
- When baking cake substitute apple sauce for oil; the cake comes out moist and tastes almost the same
- If a glass pan is used for baking, reduce the recommended oven temperature by 25 degrees
- Instant potatoes work well as a thickener for homemade stews
- Vegetables that grow above ground should be boiled with no cover
- Cut meat across the grain before cooking to make it easier to eat after cooking

- While the pan is still hot after cooking, rinse with water and scrap off anything left with the spoon or spatula used earlier
- The quality and freshness of an egg can be checked by placing it in a bowl of cold water. If it floats it is not fresh.
- To soften brown sugar place the brown sugar in an airtight container with a slice of fresh bread placed on top or sprinkle a few drops of water or place a few apple slices over the chunk of hardened sugar, place in a plastic bag, seal, and let sit for a couple days. It should be soft and fresh again in the morning, if not just let it sit another day or two
  - Non emergency time; need the sugar soft now? Put the brown sugar in a container and place in the microwave with a small bowl full of water beside it. Microwave for about 1 minute; check. If it's still hard, try for another 30 seconds.

- Instant Non-Fat Dry Powdered Milk
  - If the Instant Nonfat Dry Milk it is stored in a cool and dry place it will retain most of its nutritional value for at least 20 years. As it sits for a long time the flavor declines - it will not be as noticeable if it is used as a dry ingredient in baking.
  - The flavor and texture of instant nonfat dry milk can be improved by mixing it with hot water, to completely dissolve and blend, chilling it overnight in the refrigerator.
  - To make it taste even better add real milk to the mix at a 1:10 ratio. You can use whole milk or condensed milk or evaporated milk.

o Also adding a little vanilla extract or a little granulated sugar or add a little chocolate flavoring helps enhance the flavor of old powdered milk.

Homemade Items and Substitutions

Sometimes store bought items may not be readily available but are still needed. Here are a few recipes that can be used in a pinch.

- 1 tsp. baking powder = 1/4 tsp. baking soda + 1/2 tsp. cream tartar + 1/4 tsp. Cornstarch
- 1 tsp. baking powder = 1/3 tsp. baking soda + 1/2 tsp. cream tartar
- 1 cup butter = 1 cup shortening + 1/2 tsp. Salt
- 1 tbsp. oil = 1 tbsp. melted shortening or lard
- 1 cup corn syrup = 1 cup honey = 1 cup sugar + 1/2 cup of the liquid used in the recipe
- 1 cup buttermilk = 1 cup milk + 1 tbsp. vinegar or lemon juice
- 1 cup nonfat milk = 1/3 cup nonfat dry milk + 1 cup water
- 1 cup whole milk = 1/3 cup nonfat dry milk + 1 cup water + 2 tbsp. melted butter
- 1 cup whole milk = 1/2 cup evaporated milk + 1/2 cup water
- 1 cup sugar = 1 cup corn syrup (decrease recipe liquid by 1/4 cup)
- 1 cup sugar = 1 cup honey (decrease recipe liquid by 1/4 cup)

Baby Formula (8 ounce bottle)
- 6 tbsp. nonfat dry milk
- tsp. olive or vegetable oil
- 1 tsp. Sugar
- 1 cup boiled water

Mix well. Serve at room temperature or slightly warmed. *Do not* use corn syrup or honey instead of the sugar; they both contain potential bacteria which can kill a young baby who does not have a fully developed immune system
.

Baking Powder
- 1/2 tsp. Cream of Tartar
- 1/4 tsp. Baking Soda
- 1/4 tsp. Cornstarch

Blend and measure as normal. If you do not have Cornstarch - increase the Baking Soda to 1/3 tsp

Bisquick Mix
- 3 cups flour
- 4 tsp. granulated sugar
- 1 tsp. Salt
- 1/2 cup shortening
- 1 tbsp. baking powder

Mix everything together and use in place of Bisquick Mix

Brown sugar
- 1 cup sugar
- 1 tbsp molasses

Blend together. If you prefer a darker shade of brown sugar, add an additional 1 tbsp. molasses and continue to mix until well blended.

Condensed Milk, Sweetened
- 1 cup instant nonfat dry milk
- 2/3 cup granulated sugar
- 1/3 cup boiling water
- 1/4 cup butter, melted (optional)

Combine all ingredients and mix until smooth. If the butter is omitted, then increase the water to 1/2 cup and increase the sugar to 3/4 cup. Refrigerate for up to 5 days.

Electrolyte Beverage (Gatorade, Pedialyte)
- 1 quart water
- 1 tsp. salt
- 1/2 tsp. baking soda
- 6 to 10 tsp. granulated sugar
- Flavoring (optional)

Mix well. Replaces lost electrolytes (minerals) due to dehydration from excessive exercise and sweating or diarrhea, vomiting, etc.

Hop Yeast
- 1 tsp. Hops
- 1 large potato, diced
- 1 tbsp. Sugar

- 1 pint pure water (No Chlorine)
- 1 tbsp. flour
- 1 glass bottle

Bring the cut up potato to a boil. Add the hops. Boil for 20 minutes. Strain liquid into a medium, sterile bowl and let cool slightly, add flour and sugar. Mix well. Bottle and cork tightly. The yeast should work in a few hours if you use an unwashed but recently opened beer or wine bottle. A new or washed bottle will take about 24 hours.

Mayonnaise
- egg yolks
- cups salad oil
- tbsp. lemon juice
- 1 tsp. dry mustard
- 1/8 tsp. Cayenne pepper (optional)

Mix egg yolks with dry mustard and cayenne. Stir in lemon juice. Combine the oil with the mixture a few drops at a time. Once the mixture turns white add in the rest of the oil more rapidly. Optional add-in is sugar and cream or more mustard.

Pectin --Used in jelly and jam recipes
- 10 or 12 green not yet ripe, hard, sour apples

Do not peel the apples. Cut the apples into quarters. Place in a large pot; add water to barely cover the apples.

Let simmer, covered until the apples are fully cooked. Stir every 15 – 20 minutes until the mixture looks like runny applesauce.

Place cheese cloth inside a colander /strainer then pour the hot apple mash into a cloth covered strainer.

Place the strainer over another clean pot. It will take several hours for the mixture to drip through. This slimy thick liquid is the fruit pectin. Refrigerate or freeze it until it is needed.

Substitute this apple pectin in any recipe that requires a box of fruit pectin (about 1.75 ounces) by using 3 tablespoons of the apple pectin combine with 4 tablespoons sugar.

Self-Rising Flour
- 1 cup flour
- 1/2 tsp. Salt
- 1/2 tbsp. baking powder

Mix together and place in a cool, dry spot in an air tight container.

Sour Cream
- 1 cup instant nonfat dry milk
- 1/2 cup warm water
- 1 tbsp. vinegar or lemon juice

Add the dry milk to the warm water in a bowl and stir until completely dissolved. Slowly add the vinegar a few drops at a time and continue stirring. Sour cream will thicken as it chills.

Herbal Antibiotics

Antibiotics are used to cure bacterial infections and illnesses however antibiotics have no effect on viruses. Colds, flu and bronchitis are all viral. Viruses survive only inside of the body as bacteria organisms are found both inside and outside of the body.

Some kinds of bacteria are actually beneficial in protecting our bodies against the harmful ones. Antibiotics kill off *all* bacteria and cannot decipher between the good and bad, making our immune system compromised. Without the healthy protection from good bacteria, any bad bacteria left can now readily multiply and take hold.

Your immune system can effectively fight off viruses and pathogenic bacteria with the use of natural organic herbal antibiotics. These herbs, which are well known to have antibiotic properties, are to be taken at the initial signs of an illness. These herbs will help the body heal itself. The most effective herbs that have an effect on the body's immune system are Sage, Garlic, Calendula, Goldenseal, Thyme, Peppermint, Neem, Licorice, Basil, Thyme, and Echinacea.

Of these, Echinacea, Goldenseal and Calendula have a *direct effect* on the immune system. Thyme and Cayenne (warming spice/herbs) aid the immune system with their *antiseptic* properties. The herb Neem has been shown in studies to be effective at killing fourteen types of fungi, including Candida. Neem has also been recorded to suppress certain strains of Staphylococcus and Salmonella.

Lavender essential oil is known for its anti-inflammatory, antibacterial and antifungal properties.

Lavender has also been known to improve stomach disorders, digestive problems, constipation, headaches, insomnia and skin problems.

Ginger, Onion and Grapefruit seed are not herbs but are very potent immune system aids. Grapefruit seed extract has great antibacterial, antimicrobial and antifungal properties. Grapefruit seeds have been known to fight more than 800 different kinds of bacteria and more than 100 different kinds of fungi. Grapefruit seeds destroy bad bacteria without destroying the good bacteria in the body.

Garlic *is* in the herb family and contains a natural compound known as Allici, which is more powerful than Penicillin. Garlic does a very good job at fighting infections both inside and outside of the body. It can be taken orally to fight bacterial infections, such as a sore throat infection, ear infection, sinus infection, kidney infection, bladder infection, etc. It can be used as an external topical application as it kills fungal infections like vaginal yeast infections, athlete's foot, and oral thrush. Garlic is also an effective treatment against E. coli bacteria and staphylococcus.

Licorice root tea may help reduce ulcer symptoms, canker sores and body fat.

During the growing season the herbs can be picked, used fresh in your cooking or dried. Place the dried herbs in a jar with a screw on tight lid. Some of the dried leaves can be used as tea.

In your herb garden go ahead and let a few of the plants go to seed. Collect, label and date the envelopes and bank them as you would your other seeds for next year.

Chapter Seven

How to Grow Vegetable from Seed and Companion Planting

Every survivalist highly suggest that to be prepared for a long term event and/or to be sustainable and less dependent on anyone else, you will need to have a garden. For obvious reasons, this garden will add nutrients to your table and be a necessary part of your future supply of fresh greens.

You do not need a lot of land or space. Use pots or a raised garden patch. Place a small batch of herbs with your pansies, climbing sweet peas along side of the morning glory, cabbage with your marigolds and onions with the forget-me-nots. The best gardeners learn through experience, so dig in...literally.

"If we all did the things we are capable of doing, we would literally astound ourselves."
-Thomas A. Edison

Growing Types

Annual: They grow from seed to seed in one year. Plant dies and new plant grows from dropped seed each year.

Biennial: They grow from seed to seed in two years. New seed must be planted each year to produce a crop to eat, but it takes two years for the plant to yield seeds.

Perennial: The plants roots remain in the ground and continue to produce a new plant year after year. Seeds may be produced after two years.

Companion planting helps the plants to achieve the most from the soil - competition for nutrients and space. Some larger plants will block out sunlight to smaller plants or planting in close proximity will create a slight change in flavor.

Alphabetized List of Vegetables

1.	Asparagus	17.	Okra
2.	Beans	18.	Onion
3.	Beets	19.	Parsley
4.	Broccoli	20.	Peanuts
5.	Brussels	21.	Peas
6.	Cabbage	22.	Peppers
7.	Carrots	23.	Potatoes
8.	Cauliflower	24.	Pumpkin
9.	Celery	25.	Radish
10.	Chives	26.	Rhubarb
11.	Corn	27.	Rutabaga
12.	Cucumber	28.	Spinach
13.	Eggplant	29.	Squash
14.	Leeks	30.	Swish Chard
15.	Lettuce	31.	Tomato
16.	Melon	32.	Turnip

Asparagus: Perennial, Male and female plants; only female will yield the red seed berries when they turn red and their fern-like top leaves flop over they are ready to harvest seeds.

- Cut the berry stalk off the plant and hang it upside-down for a week to dry
- Remove the berries, soak in a bowl of water for an hour and remove the seed
- Dry the seed on a paper towel for ten days, place in a marked paper envelope, keep in a dry, cool place
- Asparagus grown from seed takes three years to produce asparagus for consumption. It will then produce asparagus each year after that
- Best when planted next to Tomatoes, Parsley and Nasturtiums

Beans: Annual, self-pollinating. Harvest the beans you wish to eat. Plant may continue to produce until the first frost.

- To gather seeds, leave the bean pods on the best looking, most productive and earliest bearing plants. When the bean pods begin to turn brown and the beans rattle inside its pod - the beans are ready to be harvested for seed
- Place in a paper, cloth, or plastic bag
- Do not store beans in an airtight container
- Plant the beans the following spring after the last frost
- Different bean varieties should be planted at least 150 feet apart
- Best when they are planted next to Strawberries, Petunias, Rosemary, Savory, Potatoes, Carrots, Corn and Parsnips
- Do not plant next to Onions, Beets and Chives

Beets: Biennial, cross-pollinated

- Plant some beets to consume each year, and plant some beets to save through the winter to produce seed the second year
- Plant the beet seeds you intend to keep through the winter in the early summer so the beets don't grow too large the first year
  - Examine them as they grow, discard any that have poor leaf quality
  - The beet will produce a rosette of flowers the first year but no seeds. If a beet produces a seed bolt the first year dig discard it
  - If you have short mild winters, you may leave the beets in the ground all winter
  - If the winter months are bitter then dig up the beets before the first fall frost and save 5-10 beets that have the best quality roots. Leave one-inch of the top of the beet greens
  - Bury the beets in damp sand or sawdust in a cool humid area for the winter
  - Do not let it freeze. Inspect the beets the following spring and discard any beets that withered
- Replant the good beets with their crowns just below the dirt at about eighteen inches apart
- They will grow and produce a tall seed stalk with tiny blossoms
- Seed balls will contain five or six seeds each
- When the seed balls begin to turn brown they are ready for harvest. Cut off the seed stalk, hang it indoors upside down, remove the seeds and store in a labeled paper envelope in a dry, cool area
- Do not plant beets in the same exact area two years in a row. Rotate your beet crop with

either corn or potatoes to maximize the yield
from your soil
- Best when planted next to onions
- Do not plant next to beans

Broccoli: Annual, contain male and female parts,
pollinated by insects.
- You will need at least three plants of the same
  type for good cross-pollination
- When the head of the mature broccoli turns
  yellow, the seeds will appear within each
  flower bud inside a mature seed pod
- Harvest the seed pods and store indoors for 10
  days Place the seed pods inside a paper or
  plastic bag and carefully crush the pods using
  your hands
- Pour the contents of the bag onto a screen and
  shake the screen to separate the chaff from the
  seed
- Store the seed in a paper or cloth bag in a dry,
  cool area
- Plant next to Chamomile, Zinnias, Mint,
  nasturtiums, Chives
- Do not plant next to Strawberries

Brussels: Biennial, male and female parts, pollinated
by insects.
- The seed collection procedure is the same as
  cabbage (next vegetable below) except Brussels
  sprouts are very hardy and they may be left in
  the ground over the winter in all but severe
  winter climates
- There is also no need to slash the top of the
  Brussels sprouts for the seed stalk to appear
- Best when planted next to Chamomile, Zinnias,
  Mint

- Do not plant next to Strawberries

Cabbage: Biennial with flowers that have both the male and female parts, pollinated by insects.
- Easily cross-pollinates with many different vegetables
- At the end of the first growing season, dig up the best cabbages being careful NOT to damage their root system
- Trim off the outer leaves of each cabbage head and store the entire cabbage plant in a well ventilated cool humid area
- The cabbage must be kept cool during the winter so it will bolt the following year
- Inspect periodically during the winter and immediately discard any heads that begin to rot
- The next spring plant the cabbages by themselves at least 200 feet from all other vegetables and all other varieties of cabbage. Plant the cabbages about 30 inches apart and slightly deeper than they were planted the previous year
- Immediately after replanting, you will need to cut a one-inch deep "X" into the top center of each cabbage head to provide space for the seed stalk to rise
- The leaves grown during the second year will be smaller than the first year. If one of the cabbages shows signs of producing a poor quality seed stalk, dig it up and discard the entire cabbage so it doesn't pass its inferior pollen on to the other good cabbages
- The cabbage seed stalk will grow about five-feet tall and it will need to be supported between two stakes. Each seed stalk will contain branches of bright yellow flowers

which will produce brown seed pods containing as many as 20 seeds each

- When the seed pods turn yellow, cut off the entire seed stalk and place it on a large newspaper or cloth sheet.
- Put the remaining seed pods into a bag and carefully crush them using your hands to separate the seeds from the pods.
- Shake the seeds on a screen to separate the seeds from the chaff
- Store the seeds in a paper envelope or cloth bag in a dry, cool area
- Plant next to Rosemary, Sage, thyme, Nasturtiums, Chamomile, Zinnias, Mint, Tomatoes

Carrots: Biennial with flowers that have both the male and female parts, cross-pollinated by insects. Only plant one carrot variety per year or plant different varieties at least 1,000 feet apart.

- Leave the carrots in the ground all winter if mild
- If the winters are harsh - dig up the best quality root carrots before the first fall frost
- Cut all but one-inch off the top of the carrot greens and place the carrots sideways in a container and bury the carrots beneath damp sand or sawdust in a cool but not below freezing humid area
- Next spring replant the carrots 18 inches apart with the crown just below the surface of the earth. Pack the dirt tightly around the carrot
- The seed stalk will grow and produce flowers on a branched stalk. The seeds ripen from the top to the bottom of the stalk -- Tie small nylon bags made from old nylon hose around the seed heads so the seeds can breathe and

continue to ripen. As the seeds mature they will fall into the nylon bag and not be lost

- Shake the seeds on a screen to remove the chaff. Store the seeds in a paper envelope or cloth bag in a dry, cool area
- Best when planted next to Chives, Tomatoes, Peas, Lettuce, Beans and most Herbs
- Do not plant next to Dill

Cauliflower: Biennial with flowers that have both the male and female parts, cross-pollinated by insects with many other vegetables.

- Plant at least 200 feet from all other vegetables and other cauliflower varieties
- Plant seeds in very late spring or early summer so the cauliflower plants mature in the fall just before the first frost.
- Dig up your best cauliflower plants at the end of the first growing season and be careful that you do not damage their root system
- Store them upside down in a cool area during the winter with their roots facing up.
- The next spring plant them 30 inches apart
- They will yield a tall seed stalk containing yellow flowers and yellow seed pods
- When the seed pods turn brown, cut the seed stalk from the top of the cauliflower and lay it on a newspaper or cloth sheet so the seed pods can continue to dry and fall onto the sheet
- Store in a paper envelope in a dry, cool area
- Best when plant next to Chamomile, Zinnias and Mint
- Do not plant next to Strawberries

Celery: Biennial with flowers that have both the male and female parts, cross-pollinated by insects.

- Celery requires 120 to 135 days to mature
- Dig up the best plants--careful to not damage the roots
- Replant the roots in some soil indoors and completely mulch the celery tops with straw or hay
- Store in a humid, very cold area for the winter
- Retrieve the celery plants and cut off the leaves and stalks that have rotted, and replant the celery roots outdoors 24 inches apart
- The plant will produce a bushy growth about 30 inches tall with white flowers
- The seeds will turn brown from the top to the bottom of the bush and they need to be harvested in that sequence
- Tie a nylon bag made from nylon hose around the seed heads so you can capture the seeds when the seed head shatters
- Store in a paper envelope in a dry, cool area
- Companion plant next to Leeks

Chives: Perennial, pollinated by bees, they will not cross-pollinate with other vegetables. Chives have shallow roots and weeds will choke and kill them

- If you intend to harvest the chive seeds, only harvest the outer leaves of the plant for the table
- The chives will produce round pink/purple flowers When the tiny black seeds appear they are ready to be harvested
- Cut off the seed head and dry it indoors for six weeks
- Separate the seeds with your hands and store in a paper envelope, place in a dry, cool area

- Companion plant next to Carrots, Broccoli, Lettuce and Peas
- Do not plant next to Beans

Corn: Annual with male tassels and female flowers (ears) on each plant cross-pollinated by the wind. The wind can easily carry the pollen 1,000 feet -- plant only one variety of corn to avoid mixing varieties.
- Leave the largest most perfect earliest bearing ears of corn on the stalk and harvest the rest for eating -- save the ears from different stalks to prevent future inbreeding problems
- Peel back the husks and hang the corn on their stalks upside down in a well-ventilated room for another 4 weeks to allow the corn kernels more time to ripen
- Wait until the corn kernels are hard and completely dry -- if they are not dry they will not store well
- Twist off the full kernels of corn and discard the kernels near the end of the ear that are small and only partially developed
- Store in a paper envelope in a dry, cool area
- In the spring, soak the seeds in some warm water for three hours before planting to improve their germination
- Best when planted next to Beans, Cucumber, Pumpkin, Squash, Lamb's Quarters, Potatoes, Radishes, Berries

Cucumber: Annual with male and female flowers on the same plant. The male flowers appear in groups, the female flowers have a small fruit at the base, cross-pollinated by bees so only plant one variety of cucumber per year.
- Leave the best looking cucumbers on the vine about five weeks after you have harvested the

others for eating. They will become fat and yellow
- Cut the cucumber in half and scrape the seedy interior pulp into a bowl of water.
- Stir the water occasionally--after about five days the seeds will sink to the bottom of the bowl
- Remove them, rinse them off, and place them on a screen to dry for another 10 days
- When the seed breaks instead of bends it is dry enough
- Store the seeds in a paper envelope in a dry, cool place
- Plant next Corn and Radishes

Eggplant: Annual with flowers that have both the male and female parts, self-pollinated but occasionally cross-pollinated by insects. Therefore only plant one variety per year.
- Wait for the mature fruit to drop from the plant
- Save the fruits from several different plants
- Cut the eggplant in half and scrape the seedy interior pulp into a bowl of water
- Stir the water until the seeds separate from the pulp and fall to the bottom of the bowl
- Remove the seeds from the bottom of the water, rinse, and dry on screens or paper towels
- The seed is dry enough when it does not bend
- Store the seeds in a paper envelope in a dry, cool area

Leeks: Biennial, cross-pollinated by insects. Different varieties of leek should be planted at least 200 feet apart.

- Remove the smaller plants and leave the larger, higher quality leeks in the ground during the winter. If the winters are long and bitter, then cover with a layer of mulch
- When left in the ground, leeks will form small bulbs around the base of the plant the following spring
- These bulbs can be removed and planted to yield a fresh crop of leeks
- During the second growing season a tall stalk will appear with a ball of tiny flowers at its tip
- When the seeds form inside the small paper thin capsules they are ready to be harvested
- Cut off the entire seed stalk and place it indoors inside a bag to dry
- Store the seeds in a paper envelope or cloth bag in a dry, cool area
- Plant next to Celery

Lettuce: Annual with flowers that have both the male and female parts, self-pollinating. Lettuce prefers cool weather and it will go to seed (bolting) when the days are long and hot.

- Lettuce that is allowed to bolt should be separated by 12 inches from one another
- One lettuce plant can produce as many as 30,000 seeds. The seeds do not ripen at the same time. Instead they ripen over a period of 4 to 8 weeks
- When some of the seeds have turned dark, shake those dark seeds into a paper bag. Allow to dry indoors for another seven days

- Store the seeds in a paper envelope in a dry, cool area.
- Plant lettuce seeds slightly under the top soil the following spring
- Plant next to Carrots, Chives, Garlic, Radishes, Strawberries, Zinnias, tall plants for shade

Melons: Annual with male and female flowers on the same plant, cross-pollinated by insects. Do not plant within 200 feet of any other variety of melon.
- When the melon is ripe enough to eat, the seeds are also ready for harvesting
- Cut the melon and scrape out the seedy interior pulp into a bowl of water
- Stir gently and the heavy seeds will settle to the bottom of the bowl
- Remove the seeds, rinse, and dry thoroughly on a screen or paper towel
- When the seed breaks instead of bending it is dry enough
- Store the seeds in a paper envelope in a dry, cool place
- In the spring place the seeds between two moist paper towels and then place inside a plastic bag in a warm place
- When the seeds germinate, plant the tiny seedlings

Okra: Annual, self-pollinating. Only plant one variety per year.

- Okra's yellow flowers have a red center which is followed by a pod
- Before the pod is fully developed it is harvested for eating
- To yield seed, the pods must be left on the plant until they turn woody in the fall and then they are harvested
- Crack open the pods and harvest the seeds
- Let dry and place in a paper envelope and store in a dry, cool place.

Onions: Biennial, cross-pollinated by insects

- Different varieties should be planted at least 1,000 feet apart during their second year
- If an onion bolts to seed the first year, do not save the seeds
- Dig up the onions in the fall and save the best quality onions in a well ventilated dry, cool area above freezing for the winter
- The next spring cut a shallow "X" in the top of each onion to provide an area for the seed stalk to emerge
- Then replant the onions 4 inches apart and cover with 1/2 inch of soil
- During the summer a tall seed stalk will appear with a round flower head which will yield black seeds
- When the seeds begin to appear cut off the seed stem and dry it indoors for six weeks to allow time for the seeds to mature
- Remove the seeds. Store the seeds in a paper envelope in a dry, cool area
- Onions have the best eating quality and flavor when grown from seed

- Best when planted next to Radishes, Chamomile, Savory, Beets, Berries, Tomatoes and Chard
- Do not plant next to Peas and Beans

Parsley: Biennial with flowers that have both the male and female parts, cross-pollinated by insects. Do not plant different parsley varieties the same year.

- Don't save the seeds from parsley that bolts to seed the first year
- For a continuous supply of parsley, plant every two weeks through mid-summer
- After the first few frosts in the fall, cover the parsley with leaves, hay, or straw for the winter. Uncover them in the early spring
- During the second growing season, parsley will produce tall branching flower stalks that yield lots of seeds.
- The seed heads ripen slowly so tie a nylon bag made from nylon hose around the seed stalks to catch the seeds when the flower heads burst in the fall
- Harvest the seed stalks before the first frost and shake inside a paper bag to remove any additional seeds
- Store the seeds in a paper envelope in a dry, cool area
- Parsley seeds will form a germination-inhibiting coating which should be removed prior to planting
- To remove the coating, soak the seeds in some warm water for two days the following spring. Change the water every 12 hours and rinse the seeds once more just before planting
- Good next to Tomatoes and/or Asparagus

Peanut: Annual, self-pollinating, only plant one variety per year. Peanuts grow in clusters underground.

- When the above ground leaves turn yellow, dig up the entire plant and store indoors for an additional four weeks in a cool, dry area
- Leave the peanuts inside their shells until you are ready to eat them or use them for seed
- If you shell them for seed, be very careful to not break or tear the pink paper thin seed coat around the peanut
- Plant the peanut inside its thin seed coat for the best germination results

Peas: Annual. Self-pollinating but occasionally cross-pollinated by bees so plant different varieties at least 100 feet apart. Peas do not do well when transplanted; plant peas during the last week of winter or first week of spring as they are hardy plants and can survive spring frosts.

- Put a layer of mulch close around your plants to help shade the roots and keep the soil cool
- Inspect your mature plants and select the strongest, earliest bearing plants with the heaviest set of peas
- Allow the peas on those plants to remain inside their seed pods until they are really dry and you can hear them rattle inside their seed pods
- Remove the seeds from their pods by hand
- Store in a paper envelope in a dry, cool place
- The following spring *before* the last frost, soak the peas in some warm water for three hours before planting outdoors
- Poke your finger into the soft earth about 1.5" and drop the pea into the hole

- Do not cover the hole with dirt. Late snows or early spring rains will fill the hole and provide the additional moisture the peas need to germinate
- Plant next to Carrots, Chives, Radishes and/or Garlic
- Peas do not do well next to onions

Pepper: Annual with flowers that have both the male and female parts Self-pollinating. However, bees will transport the pollen among plants so different varieties should be planted at least 50 feet apart.

- Due to their long growing season pepper seeds need to be started indoors about 8 weeks before the last frost the next spring
- Keep the soil very warm and water the soil sparingly during this 8 week period
- Too much nitrogen fertilizer will produce strong healthy bushes but yield minimum fruits
- Harvest most of the peppers when they are ready to eat but leave the healthiest best looking peppers on the vine
- Wait for the peppers to change color and begin to shrivel.
- Save the peppers from several different plants
- If frost is forecast and the peppers have not yet changed color, then bring them indoors and wait for the seed to ripen
- If pepper seeds are not allowed to fully ripen they will NOT germinate well the following spring
- Cut the fully ripe shriveled peppers and remove the inner cluster of seeds
- Place the seeds on a paper towel and allow them to dry for 14 days

- When the seed breaks when you apply pressure
- Store in a paper envelope or cloth bag in a dry, cool area Pepper seeds germinate best in warm dry soil
- Do not plant where tobacco has grown in the past or near where it is currently growing

Potato: Annual, self-pollinated; typically grown from the eyes of the potato or the small sprouts that appear on a mature potato as it ages.

- Potatoes should be stored in a cool area over the winter at a temperature above 45°F
- Small potatoes the size of an egg or a little larger should be planted whole
- Potatoes smaller than an egg should be discarded
- Large potatoes with eight or more eyes should be cut into pieces with one to three eyes per piece, leave as much potato as possible on each piece
- Allow the cuts to heal and dry for two days before planting
- Too many eyes on a potato will yield a large above ground plant but very few potatoes below ground
- Plant the cut side facing down about 3 inches deep and about 10 inches apart
- When the green tops are about 8 inches high, cover them with some more soil or hay
- Harvest the potatoes as you need them
- Most gardeners who experiment with potato seeds have not experienced good results
- Best when planted next to Beans, Corn, Horseradish, Dead nettle and Flax

- Does not do well next to Squash, Tomatoes and Sunflowers

Pumpkins: Annual with male and female flowers on the same plant, cross-pollinated by insects. The female flower has a tiny fruit at its base whereas the male flower does not.
- Plant different varieties at least 500 feet apart
- Pumpkins seeds will be ripe at the same time that the pumpkin is ready to be harvested and eaten
- Cut the pumpkin open, scrape the seedy pulp into a bowl of water, and separate the seeds from the pulp
- Examine the seeds and discard the flat ones
- Spread the plump seeds onto a paper towel and allow drying for 10 days
- Store in a paper envelope in a dry, cool area
- Does well next to Corn
- But not too close to Potato plants

Radish: Annual with tiny flowers that have both the male and female parts. Only plant one variety of radishes per year to avoid cross-pollination. The flowers will not produce seed during very hot or very dry weather.
- Harvest the radishes when they are ready to eat
- Select the most desirable ones to use to produce seed
- Cut all but one-inch off the top of the radish green leaves
- Replant the radishes with their crowns level with the soil, at about 8 inches apart
- Pull up and discard the first radishes to bolt

- The radishes that bolt to seed later will produce the best seed
- The two or three feet tall green seed pods will first turn yellow and then brown
- Pull up the entire plant, hang them in a well ventilated area and allow drying
- Crush the seed pods by hand to remove the seeds
- Store the seeds in a paper envelope in a cool, dry area
- Companion plant next to Corn, peas, lettuce, Geraniums, Nasturtiums, Onions, Chervil, Cucumbers
- Does not do well near potatoes

Rhubarb: Perennial, cross-pollinated by insects, needs a cold climate to do well.
- Rhubarb seeds will appear on a tall seed stalk that appears in the summer
- When the top of the seed stalk becomes dry and flaky, cut it off and then remove and dry the seeds
- The seeds produced may not result in a copy of the parent plant
- It is better to propagate by dividing the crown of the rhubarb and replanting them instead

Rutabaga: Biennial with flowers that have both the male and female parts, pollinated by insects.
- Rutabagas should be planted earlier than turnips because they grow slower, such as early August. Follow the planting and seed collection directions for turnips

Spinach: Annual, wind pollinated and cross-fertilization is possible with any other variety planted within one mile.

- Plant the spinach every two weeks to have a continuous supply. Spinach prefers cool weather during very early spring or during the late summer
- The best plants to use for seeds are the ones that are the last to bolt; it is a longer producer of leaves
- When the spinach leaves begin to turn yellow, pull up the plant and remove the seeds by hand
- Dry the seeds for 14 days and then store in a paper envelope in a dry, cool spot

Squash: Annual with male and female flowers on the same plant. The female flower has a tiny fruit at its base whereas the male flower does not. They can be cross-pollinated by insects so plant different varieties at least 500 feet apart.

- Winter squash seeds are harvested at the same time the winter squash is ready to be eaten
- Hang it up indoors for an additional six weeks to dry
- Summer squash is to remain on the vine for eight weeks after harvest, cut the squash in half, separate the seeds from the pulp and place into a bowl of water - discard the flat ones
- Spread the plump seeds onto a paper towel and dry for 10 days
- The seed is dry enough when it breaks instead of bends
- Store the seeds in a paper envelope in a dry, cool area

Swish Chard: Biennial with male and female part flowers and cross-pollinated by the wind. The tall seed stalks will appear the second year and need to be staked.

- The plant may be left in the ground during the first winter
- Place a layer of mulch or compost over the top
- When the seed stalk becomes dry, remove its seeds and dry them indoors
- Store the seeds in a paper envelope in a dry, cool area
- Companion plant next to onions

Tomato: Annual, male and female parts to the flower, self-pollinated but insects can cross-pollinate different varieties so plant different varieties at least 10 feet apart.

- Select the best looking, earliest bearing, and most productive plants for seed collection from about three different plants to provide for a gene pool
- To harvest the tomato seeds, pick when they are ripe
- Cut the tomatoes and scrape the seedy pulp into a shallow bowl of water
- Remove and discard any pulp and seed that floats
- Remove the seeds from the bottom of the bowl after three days
- Rinse and place on paper towels for 10 days to dry thoroughly
- Store the seed in a paper envelope in a dry, cool area
- Plant next to most Herbs, Flowers, Onions, Asparagus, Cabbage and Carrots.
- Do not plant next to Potatoes

Turnip: Biennial with male and female parts flowers; pollinated by insects.

Northern areas should plant in the midsummer and early fall planting in the southern areas.

- Choose the ones you want to go to seed next year.
- Leave those in the ground during the winter with a covering of mulch.
- On the second year thin the plants to 18 inches apart. They will produce a seed stalk the second year.
- When the seed pods turn yellow, cut off the entire seed stalk and place it on a large newspaper or cloth sheet. Some of the seeds will fall off onto the sheet.
- Put the remaining seed pods into a bag and carefully crush them using your hands to separate the seeds from the pods.
- Store the seeds in a paper envelope in cool area.

Add your favorites here

Seed Bank
Harvesting and Storing

Different plants produce seed in different forms. Fruit seeds are encased in the fruit and can be collected when the fruit is allowed to dry. The bloom is the start of the seed collection. To propagate your favorite plant - do not remove the dead flower. Let nature take its course and watch for seedpod development. Seeds develop in a papery pod after the bloom fades and pods naturally release the seed. The seed heads that are ready to open need to be collected before they drop.

Snip off the seedpods with a pair of scissors or your fingers and place in a paper bag or envelope. Plastic bags won't do for drying seeds as they do not let air flow circulate and will ruin the seeds. Be sure to write the name of the plant and the date. It's very easy to forget what seed you picked – they all start looking the same.

Always harvest your seeds when it's dry; around mid-day or early afternoon on a warm, sunny day. If the seeds are damp, collect them and place on a paper towel to dry thoroughly before putting them in their individual marked envelopes.

Once your seeds are dry you may need to get them out of their shells. Poke the pods with a thin stick to get all the seeds out so as to not waste. Some pods will need to be cut in half. To collect the seeds without all the extra bits and pieces you will need several sheets of paper.

If you would like, use a strainer to separate the seeds from the rubbish. Depending on the size of the seed use a strainer with larger holes down to a wire mesh which will allow dust and dirt to be removed.

A pair of tweezers is useful for picking up medium to larger size seeds. Seeds that are small can be separated from their chaff by holding the paper at an angle and letting the seed roll down. Doing both usually results in just seeds.

Store the seeds in a marked envelope and place the envelope in an alphabetized 'filing' box. Place the box in a dry, cool place.

Collect a few years worth of seeds as you may have a bad crop one year. Swap seeds with other gardeners for fun or use as a bartering item.

When to Plant and Hardiness Zones

Suggested hardiness zones have been indicated for most trees and perennials. Most have a zone range. Suitable hardiness means a plant can be expected to grow in the zone's temperature extremes. Keep in mind that local variations such as moisture, soil, winds, and other conditions might affect the viability of individual plants. You may want to ask a local professional or nursery about which plants and trees to plant in your community.

With warm weather many people became anxious to plant. There is a common wisdom of planting by holidays and a science behind it. The holiday rule of thumb is to plant peas and lettuce on St. Patrick's Day and peppers and tomatoes on Memorial Day.

You can make the decisions on planting dates based on risk tolerance. In some years early planting may prove to be a good bet and in others, a disaster.

Soil temperatures

Cool season vegetables –
35 degrees - lettuce and onions
40 degrees – peas, radishes, spinach, cabbage

Warm season vegetables –
50 degrees – tomato, peppers, corn
55 degrees – beans
60 degrees – cucumbers, squash, eggplant

The science behind this is that cool season vegetables are planted when soil temperatures are sufficiently warm for seed germination. These vegetables are able to withstand cold air temperatures. Warm season vegetables require warmer soil temperatures for seed germination and root growth, and warm air temperatures for plant tops. Many but not all warm season vegetables are planted as transplants and not directly into the outdoor ground.

The USDA Hardiness Zone Map divides North America into 11 areas based on a 10 degree Fahrenheit difference in the average annual minimum temperature. The United States falls within Zones 2 through 10. Before you plant anything, look up your Hardiness Zone to be sure your garden thrives.

Chapter Eight

Survival Skills

The main idea for preparation is to create a well stocked supply of food and non-food survival items. By supplementing your canned food form the grocery store with jarred food from your garden, the supply will last a lot longer. Now add hunting and fishing to the canned meat supply and foraging wild plants; the variety and ongoing sustainability of your food has gone up exponentially.

All this is subjective to the facts of the disaster. If the disaster is a flood, your canned food is still edible and depending on if your dry food supply has been packaged correctly and water will not get into the container your food supply will be intact. But if the disaster is a fire, most likely the plastic will melt and the canned food has burst. Hopefully, if the disaster is a wildfire, you will have some warning and be able to evacuate with most of your supply. If the area is affected by a major event, your supplies may be destroyed and of little use

"It's not whether you get knocked down; it's whether you get up." - Vince Lombardi
Influential American football coach - 1913 - 1970

Along with taking a proactive approach to preparedness with food storage, you need to know the skills of survival, not only for the short term events but for the potential long term catastrophic events.

You already have some skills that others do not and you have the chance to pass on your skill to the next generation. There are always new things to learn, practice and research. But just in case the need arises and a skill is not readily available to be taught, then books are the next best thing. An extensive library for reference and entertainment is not only a luxury but a necessity.

The following 'How to..." list is set up to be very basic. It will cover skills needed to attain some sustainability before and after a disaster hits. This list is *not* complete for the deep survivalist. That list would include things like how to build a cabin cave, how to make bio-diesel fuel, homemade solar and wind power for your home and a lot more. (See Survival of the Prepared, Vol. II)

But, as it is, we have the technology and electricity now, so now is the time to purchase items that are still available and much easier to obtain than after an emergency. It is easier to learn now with items you have on hand, then to make them from scratch. However, it is always good to *know* how to survive without the electronics and convenience of modern times.

It will be much more fun to learn from a mistake *now*. Now's the time to try the "live and learn" skill set. Don't wait until others may be depending on you to provide food and shelter.

How To...Make, Create, Construct and/or Build...

The list is alphabetized for easy searching.

1. Bread
2. Brine
3. Butter
4. Campfire
5. Candles
6. Candle Wicks
7. Ferment, Lacto-
8. Fire sticks
9. Glue
10. Hard Cider
11. Jerky
12. Lard, Render
13. Pemmican
14. Solar Box Oven
15. Sourdough Starter
16. Sprouts
17. Whey
18. Yogurt

How to Make

Bread from Scratch

Have you ever made a loaf of yeast bread or some yeast rolls? If not, take a little time and try it. Bread making is actually quite easy once you learn some basic techniques, and nothing smells as wonderful as baking bread. Bread machines are wonderful, but knowing how to make yeast bread recipes from scratch will boost your self-confidence when you may need to make the bread and a meal without the aid of electricity.

Yeast

Make sure your yeast is fresh. Use the 'best if used by' date on the packages. Active dry yeast, sold in individual packets are the easiest type to use and will keep well in your pantry. Cake yeast, if you can find it, really makes a wonderful loaf of bread. This form of yeast is fresh, stored in the refrigerator but is very perishable.

When the yeast is dissolved in the water, the temperature must be 110° to 115°. The temperature of the water, whether used to dissolve the yeast, or added to a yeast/flour mixture, is critical. Until you get some experience, use a thermometer.

Flour

The flour you choose for your bread also makes a difference in the quality of the final product. Bread flour makes a superior loaf. This flour is higher in protein content. Protein, or gluten, is what gives bread its unique texture. When water is added to flour, the two proteins, glutenin and gliadin combine to form gluten.

Gluten forms a network of proteins that stretch through the dough like a web, trapping air bubbles that form as the yeast ferments. Whole grain flours and other types of flour add color, texture, and flavor to breads. These flour types don't have enough gluten to make a successful loaf on their own, so all purpose or bread flour is almost always added to provide structure.

Do not use cake flour - there isn't enough protein and your bread will fall; the structure won't be able to withstand the pressure of the gasses the yeast creates. All purpose flour will also work just fine in most bread recipes.

Liquid

The type of liquid you use will change the bread characteristics. Water will make a loaf that has more wheat flavor and a crisper crust. Milk and cream-based breads are richer, with a finer texture. These breads brown more quickly because of the additional sugar and butterfat added to the dough.

Orange juice is a nice addition to whole wheat breads because its sweetness helps counter the stronger flavor of the whole grain.

Fats

Fats like oils, butter and shortening add tenderness and flavor to bread. Breads made with these ingredients are generally moister. Make sure you do not use whipped butter or margarine, or low fat products, since they contain water. The composition of the dough will be weakened, and your loaf will fall.

Eggs

Eggs add richness, color, and flavor to the dough and resulting bread. Egg breads have a wonderful flavor.

Sugar

Sugar is the fuel that feeds yeast so it ferments, producing carbon dioxide that makes the bread rise. Some bread recipes don't use sugar, but depend on sugars in the flour to provide food for the yeast.

Salt

Salt is essential to every bread recipe. It helps control yeast development, and prevents the bread from over rising.

This contributes to good texture. Salt also adds flavor to the bread. It is possible to make salt-free breads, but if doing so, other ingredients like vinegar or yogurt are added to help control the yeast growth.

Toppings

Toppings can change the crust of the loaf. Egg glazes are used to attach other ingredients like nuts or seeds. An egg yolk glaze will create a shiny, golden crust. Egg white glazes make a shiny, crisp crust. For a chewy, crisp crust, spray the dough with water while it's baking. When you brush milk or butter on the dough before baking, the crust will be soft and tender.

Measure

Measure the liquid and heat it to the correct temperature. Sprinkle the yeast over the liquid, and let this sit for a few minutes. This is called proofing the yeast, and ensures that the yeast is fresh and active. When the yeast mixture rises and starts bubbling, proceed with the rest of the bread recipe. Measure part of the flour into a bowl, and add any other dry ingredients or flavorings.

Mix Ingredients

Make a depression in the center of the flour then add the dissolved yeast and other liquids along with eggs, if used in the recipe. Beat well to combine. Gradually add the rest of the flour until the bread dough becomes difficult to stir. At this point, flour your work surface and dump the dough out of the bowl onto the floured surface. Gather the dough into a rough ball, adding more flour as necessary so your fingers don't stick to the dough. Begin kneading the dough. Dough made with bread flour typically require more kneading than those made with all purpose flours.

Knead the Dough

To knead, turn the dough over several times, gathering any stray particles. Fold the dough in half towards you, and push away with the heels of your hands.

Turn the dough one quarter turn, and repeat this process until the dough is smooth, elastic, springy, and no longer sticky. Sprinkle more flour on the dough as you work so it doesn't stick to the board or your hands. This process will take from 5 to 10 minutes.

Let it Rise

Grease a large mixing bowl lightly with shortening or butter. Place the smooth, kneaded dough into the bowl, turning it over so the top is greased as well. This step makes sure the dough doesn't dry out as it rises. Cover with a clean cloth and place in a warm spot. An electric oven with the light turned on, or a gas oven with the pilot light are perfect places for rising. Let the dough rise until double in bulk. This means the dough increases in size, and when you press your fingers into the top, the indentation remains when you remove your fingers.

Form the Loaves

Punch down the dough by pushing your fist into the center. Pull the edges of the dough into the depression and push it down to expel the air. Then turn it onto a floured surface. Shape according to the recipe. Place the dough in greased loaf tins, or on a greased cookie sheet for free form loaves. Cover and let rise again until double in size. This second rising will take less time, because there is more yeast in the dough.

Bake It

Bake the bread in a preheated oven. The bread should rise a bit in the oven too - this is called 'oven spring'. Bake according to the recipe until golden brown. The bread is done when it sounds hollow when you tap it with your fingers. Remove from the pans and let cool on a wire rack

Home Style Bread Recipe

Ingredients
- 1 (.25 ounce) package active dry yeast
- 2 cups warm water (110 degrees to 115 degrees)
- 1 cup sugar
- 1/2 cup butter, melted
- 1 1/2 teaspoons salt
- 2 eggs, beaten
- 7 cups bread flour

Dissolve yeast in warm water; add the sugar, butter, salt, eggs. Then add only 4 cups flour. Beat until smooth. Stir in remaining flour to form the dough. Place on a floured surface; knead until smooth and elastic, about 6-8 minutes. Place in a greased bowl, turning once to grease top. Cover the mixture and let rise in a warm place until it doubles in size. This will usually take about 1 hour. Punch dough down, place onto a floured surface. Divide into thirds. Shape into loaves and place in three greased 9-in. x 5-in. x 3-in. loaf pans. Cover and let rise again to double in size; about 1 hour. Bake at 350 degrees F for 25-30 minutes or until golden brown. Remove from pans to wire racks to cool.

How to Make Basic
Brine

Brine is a mix of salt and water which is used to start off pickling and/or a fermenting process. The basic recipe is:

1 cup salt
1 gallon water

The ratio should be between 8% - 10% weight of non-iodized salt to pure water. Mix the salt into the water. The water will appear cloudy then clear within a few minutes. Smaller batches can be made by using half and quarter amounts but make sure to keep the water/salt ratio. This brine can be poured over any vegetable ready to be fermented or pickled.

Add sugar to the mix to make sweet brine. This sweet brine is used to marinate lean cuts of meat; chicken, turkey or pork. The meat is soaked in brine for a nothing less than 8 hours otherwise the affect is not the same. The salt brine infuses the meat with its own natural flavor through the process of osmosis, the movement of water in and out of cells, thus keeping it moist. The sugar adds a different element to the flavor. Honey, brown sugar or even maple syrup can be used to change the end result. Make sure to keep an eye on the meat when broiling or grilling since the sugar will make the meat more susceptible to burning.

Sweet Brine
½ cup salt
½ cup sugar
1 quart water

How to Make
Butter

In these modern times, making your own butter is not something that you usually think about. However, life used to be much harder and this common chore had to be done to gain this small luxury. Of course, in the olden days they used a butter churn. For an emergency event, using a jar works very well.

Things You'll Need

- Clean and dried small jar with tight fitting lid
- Small kitchen towel or piece of cheesecloth
- Butter knife/Spatula
- Heavy cream

Wash and dry a small jar. Fill the jar about half way to the top with heavy cream; replace lid securely. Shake the jar with the cream in it for about 10 to 20 minutes. Once most of the liquid is gone and a large lump of butter has formed, scoop the butter out of the jar with a butter knife. Place the butter inside a clean kitchen towel or cheesecloth.

Close the kitchen towel or cheesecloth over the butter. Hang the butter ball over a jar or bowl. This extracts all of the left over liquid and leaves you only with the solid butter. Shape the butter and place it in the fridge for about 1 hour to harden. The left over liquid is a form of whey. *Whey* is the liquid remaining after milk has been curdled and strained, and can be used in making lacto-fermented fruits and vegetables.

How to Build a
Campfire for Cooking

The object is to have all your wood turn into coals at the same time. This gives an even fire with no flames that could burn your food or blacken your cookware. Remember to use cast iron for campfire cooking.

Preparing Your Fire Site

Select a fire site at least 10 feet from bushes or shrubs and be sure no tree branches are hanging over your fire site. Then make a U-shaped perimeter using large rocks or green logs. If using green logs make sure you wet them down from time to time. If it is a windy day, make sure the back of the fire pit faces the wind. Place a large flat rock at the rear of the fire pit to act as a chimney. The "chimney rock" will help direct the smoke up and away from your cooking area.

Laying the kindling

Fill the fire area with crumpled paper or tinder. Lay kindling over paper/tinder in layers, alternating direction with each layer. Use thin pieces of wood or small dead branches. Do not put kindling down in a "tepee style". The whole fire area should be covered with the kindling flat stack. Light the paper or tinder to start your fire.

Building the Fire, grading the coals

When the kindling is ablaze, add you firewood. The wood should be the same size, as much as possible. Use hardwood or hardwood branches if available. Distribute the wood evenly over fire bed. As soon as the last flames die down leaving mostly white coals, use a stick or shovel to push the coals into a higher level at the back end of the fire pit and keep a lower level at the front. This will give you "high", "medium," and "low" cook settings. Or, just level the coals to your preference.

Cooking

To cook, set a grill on rocks or wet green logs. Put food directly on grill or in cookware to prepare your meal. If cooking directly on the grill, a small spray bottle filled with water is handy for shooting down any flames that are caused by grease drippings.

How to Make
Candles

To make candles you will need the basics;
- Wax
- A container; removable or permanent
- Wick
- Double boiler or stackable pots (a large used soup or small coffee can work great)
- Heat source.

To make fancier candles you can go all out and get the aroma scented oils, the correct type of wick, the correct kind of wax for the type of candle you wish to make, so on and so forth. All that makes for really nice candles but for right now this 'how to' is for an emergency time. You may need to improvise with items you have on hand. At a time when electricity is off, you will want to save the flashlight batteries, so make and store as many candles as you can now.

There are a few different ways to obtain wax and wicks. You can buy large wax bricks and wick supply at the hobby store or gather new or used candles and renew.

The long tapered candles burn quick and waste a perfect wick in the process. Gather up all the tapered candles you can find and melt them down. Each wick can then be used for two short, thick candles.

When you combine different color wax, you may get an ugly color candle. But in an emergency, the light is what is important.

After a candle has been completely used, remove the metal plate on the bottom of the wick that holds the wick in position, this metal plate can be used over and over again.

For small free standing candle use paper or disposable cups which can then be ripped opened after the wax sets. Glass containers are great in that they can be used over and over again, the glass glows to allow more light and the wax and wick last longer in a glass container, but it can get very hot.

To prepare a container to become a candle, simply place and stabilize the wick in the center, by either attaching the small metal plate to the bottom end of the wick or tie the top of the wick to a small stir stick, straw or chop stick laid across the top. If the wick is too short to tie, use tape to attach the wick in the correct spot while the wax hardens.

To melt the wax, use a double boiler. Pour water on the bottom of the larger pot; place the second smaller pot into the larger pot. Add the crumbled, shaved or cut up pieces of wax into the smaller pot, use low to medium heat only. If a single pot is used, constantly stir the wax on low heat. Be very careful with the heat since wax becomes flammable at 300°.

When the wax has completely melted, remove it from the heat and let all boiling action stop. Slowly pour the hot wax into a prepared container. Let it cool without disturbing.

If it looks good, cut the wick to a quarter inch in height. If you do not like the look of your candle you can shave the top portion off and smooth it or remelt and do it all over again.

How to Make
Candle Wicks

A candle wick works by transporting the melted candle wax or the fuel to the flame. When the melted wax or the fuel reaches to the flame it burns and then vaporizes.

Candle wicks are generally made by braided cotton that are finely coated with wax, and have a piece of metal wire in the centre for stiffness and to generate more heat. There are also flat-braided wicks, which are mostly used for making the tapered candles and the square-braided wicks are generally meant for making larger block candles. You will need the following:

- Cotton Kite Strings or Twine
- Clothespins and Clothes line (or anything comparable)
- Table Salt
- Boric Acid
- Scissors
- Old Newspapers
- Paper and Binder Clip

Take three strips of heavy cotton yarn or string. Soak them in the liquid mixture made out of 1 cup water, 1 tablespoon of salt and 2 tablespoon of boric acid. Or if you prefer, you can use a mixture of vinegar, water and turpentine.

The cotton strips must be soaked for at least 12 hours. Take the strips out, hang on the clothes line and let dry. When dried completely, they can be braided into a single wick. Cut the strips to the length of about six inches *more* than the desired length of a candle to be made.

The next step is to **prime** the wicks. Dip the wicks into melted hot wax till saturated twice. Wicks are completely saturated when there are no more bubbles.

Remove the wicks from the hot wax by using a paperclip and dip into water. Lay them on wax paper as straight as possible. Or hang on clothes line and let dry for a few days. Soon the wicks will turn stiff. Gather wicks and place in a plastic bag.

How to
Ferment, Lacto-, recipes

The process is about the same with each recipe. Experiment with the spiciness but keep the salt ratio to insure safety. Make sure the jars are washed and dried. Select the recipe you wish to prepare. Wash and cut the vegetables, place into the jars. Mix the sea salt and water together, and if you wish, add whey. If using water and sea salt only, add 1 cup to each jar. If using water and sea salt with whey, add 1-1/4 cups to each jar. Pack the vegetables firmly into the jars. For each jar full of peeled, quartered, shredded or sliced vegetables, fill the jar with the brine up to within 1 inch of the top. If possible, place a grape or current leaf on top of the vegetables and brine. Add a weight to the top to keep the vegetables from being exposed to air, otherwise it can grow mold. I like to use a smooth stone I have washed extensively for this purpose. The process of the *lactobacilli*'s proliferation will take about three days, at which time the mixture in the jar will be bubbly. After this process has reached day three you can remove the leaf and stone. Place the lids on the jars and tighten securely. You can now move the jars to storage. Most fermented vegetables will be ready to eat in about three weeks.

Lacto-Fermented Turnips and Beets
- Turnips – peeled, quartered and sliced
- Beets – peeled, quartered and sliced
- 1 cup of pure water with 1 tablespoon of sea salt –OR– 1 cup of pure water with 1/2 tablespoon of sea salt and 4 tablespoons of homemade whey. Have additional pure water available to fill the jars to the one inch below the top.

You may use Turnips, Beets or Radishes; combined or individually jarred. Slice them into planks or chunks, cover with brine. Try these with dill seed, garlic clove, black peppercorns, small dried red chili, mustard seed and/or red pepper flakes. Turnips tend to be a bit spicy when fermented, but are great on salads.

Pickled Garlic
Peel the cloves, fill the jar and cover with brine. This mellow, garlicky, almost sweet, tangy condiment will take four or five months to ferment fully.

Cortido
- 1 large cabbage, cored and shredded
- 1 cup carrots, grated
- 2 medium onions, very finely sliced
- 1 Tablespoon dried oregano
- 1/4 – 1/2 teaspoon red pepper flakes
- Four tablespoon sea salt
- Four tablespoons whey (if not available, use an additional 1 tablespoon salt)

Mix chopped cabbage with carrots, onions, oregano, red chili flakes, sea salt and whey. Pound the mixture with a wooden meat hammer or your fist for about 10 minutes to release juices. Place something heavy like a smooth clean stone over the top of the mixture to ensure it stays submerged

Pickled Cucumbers
- 4-5 pickling cucumbers or 15-20 gherkins
- 1 tablespoon mustard seeds
- 2 tablespoons fresh dill
- 1 tablespoon sea salt
- 4 tablespoons whey (if not available, use an additional 1 tablespoon salt)
- 1 cup filtered water

Pickled cucumbers are a classic. Use whole pickling cucumbers as well as sliced regular eating cucumbers with part of the skin removed; it may become tough and bitter. Pack the jar with cucumbers, dill seed, garlic cloves, black peppercorns and maybe some sliced onion and/or mustard seed. Cover with brine and follow the guidelines above. The cucumbers often have good flavor but turn a little mushy.

Homemade Refrigerator Pickles
Made with vinegar helps retain the crunchiness but cannot be kept on the shelves or stored long term.

- 1 cup distilled white vinegar
- 1 tablespoon salt
- 2 cups white sugar
- 6 cups sliced cucumbers
- 1 cup sliced onions

Place a medium saucepan over medium heat and bring vinegar, salt and sugar to a boil until the sugar has completely dissolved. Place the cucumbers and onions in a large bowl. Pour the vinegar mixture over the vegetables. Mix everything together then transfer to clean jars with tight fitting lids and store in the refrigerator.

Spicy Carrot
- One pint jar
- 1 to 2 medium carrots
- 1/2 onion
- 2 cloves of garlic
- Half of a jalapeno

You can adjust the amount of spiciness by using different kinds of peppers; use a hotter pepper like Serrano or Habanero or a milder pepper like an Anaheim or a banana pepper. Also a pinch of red pepper flakes can be used instead of fresh peppers.
Wash the carrots but don't peel them. Slice them into long ovals by slicing on a steep diagonal to about 1/4 inch thickness. Peel and slice the garlic cloves and slice the onion longitudinally into 1/2 inch slices or into chunks. Slice the jalapeno into rings. Layer the vegetables in the jar to within an inch of the threads.

Summer Corn Relish
- Canned or fresh corn
- Green tomato; chopped
- Red bell pepper

- Onion
- Mustard Seeds

Place ingredients in a bowl, mix then fill the jar, cover with brine secure with lid and allow two or three months for the flavor to develop.

Bread and Butter (refrigerator) Pickles
- 7 cups of cucumber - sliced
- 1 cup onions – sliced
- 1 cup bell peppers – sliced
- 2 tablespoons salt
- 1 tablespoon celery seed
  Combine and let sit for a few hours – stirring occasionally – then add
    - 2 cups sugar – stir until dissolved
    - 1 cup vinegar
    - 1 tablespoon mustard seed

If you wish, add coriander seed, dill or any other spice that suits your fancy.

How to Make a
Fire Stick

While gathering wood to make a fire you may notice that there isn't a lot of kindling. You can always make a fire stick. A firestick is a branch that is a little green or a little too large to be kindling. Take a sharp knife to the piece of wood and start cutting quarter inch incisions. The size and depth depends on what you want to do. It feels like whittling but the cuts do not go all the way through. The wood spikes look like ruffled feathers after all the cuts have been made. The green branch dries quicker and the larger dried branch burns easier.

How to Make
Homemade Glue

Homemade Glue - Recipe #1
- 6 tbsp. Water
- envelopes Gelatin
- tbsp. white vinegar
- tsp. Glycerine

Boil water, remove from heat and add gelatin, vinegar and glycerin. Mix well and store in a tightly lidded jar.

Homemade Glue - Recipe #2
This glue is very effective for gluing glass to glass, metal to metal, wood, mending china and labels on glass jars. To glue items together allow glue to cool slightly so it begins to jell. Glue should be stored in a screw capped glass jar. To restore it to usefulness set jar in hot water.

- (1/2 oz.) packets unflavoured gelatin
- tbsp. cold water
- tbsp. skimmed milk
- Few drops of oil of wintergreen

In a small bowl, sprinkle gelatin into cold water. Set aside to soften. Heat milk to boiling and pour into softened gelatin. Stir until dissolved. Add oil of wintergreen as a preservative. The batch should make a little more than ½ cup. Best if used while it is still warm; apply with a brush.

How to Make
Hard Apple Cider

Hard cider, an alcoholic beverage made through fermentation of apple cider, is a delicious alternative to beer that's brewed by a similar method. Cider has been a popular alcoholic beverage in America since colonial times. While cider lost some of its popularity it has recently made a comeback with the increasing interest in microbreweries and home brewing. With just a few basic pieces of equipment and supplies, you can brew hard cider at home. Brewing cider involves the use of active yeast culture, which may cause some food allergies. Sterilize all containers and tools and use only fresh ingredients. Use un-pasteurized or raw apple cider from your local orchard – or – collect apples, smash and press to collect cider, or buy fresh, unpasteurized apple cider.

There are two basic methods:

1. Put the apple cider into a container with a vapor lock and let the wild yeast that occurs naturally in apples ferment the juice into booze. This takes 4 to 6 months and yields unpredictable results. If you want simple, it doesn't get much easier than this.

2. Pasteurize the apple cider by applying steady medium heat, boil for about ten minutes, remove from the heat and let cool. The thermometer should get down to 110° before you add brewer yeast; champagne yeast works well also. Put the cider it in a container with a vapor lock. This method takes less time at only 3 to 5 weeks to ferment and will yield a more stable cider.

How to Make

Jerky

Slice the meat into strips in the same direction as the muscle. Each strip should be about 1 inch wide and 1/4 inch thick. The length is not important. Trim off all the fat because the fat won't cure properly; it will spoil the meat. Support the meat while drying by hanging it over a clean straight pole. Or push a thin wire through one end of each piece of meat and then hang the string of meat between two trees. The most important thing is that each piece of meat should not touch itself or another strip of meat. Dry the raw meat using either one of the following two methods:

First Method:
Dry the raw meat in direct sunlight. Protect the meat strips with cheesecloth or screen wire so the birds can't eat them and the flies can't lay eggs on them. This is the method that was used by some Native American Indians. However, this method is **not** as effective as the next method.

Second Method:
The preferred method is to dry the raw meat strips over a fire. Dig a hole in the ground and start a fire in the hole. Don't use soft wood such as pine because the pine pitch will taint the meat. When the fire has burned down to hot coals, hang the meat between two stakes about two feet above the hot coals. The air should feel hot to your hand but it should not burn your hand. You do *not* want to cook the meat. You only want to dry the meat. Add a few damp hardwood chips (or some decayed wood) to the coals to make smoke.

The smoke will put a protective coating on the meat. The heat and the smoke will keep the birds and flies away. The heat will also destroy any harmful microorganisms in the meat.

Periodically bend the meat jerky strips to test for dryness. Properly dried meat jerky will crack or snap when bent. If it bends without cracking, it still contains too much moisture. If it crumbles, it is too dry. It will still be edible but it will have lost some of its nutritional value.

Store the dried meat jerky in a container to protect it from insects. Properly dried meat jerky is safe to eat for up to one year.

Write your favorite recipe here.

How to
Render Lard

While lard isn't considered a food, it was and still is vital to the cooking process. A 225-pound hog will yield about 30 pounds of fat that can be rendered into fine shortening for pastries, biscuits, and frying. A sheet of ninety percent fat sits just outside the ribs making the best quality easily rendered snowy-white lard. The back fat, a thick layer just under the skin, is almost as good, giving about eighty percent of its weight in lard.

You will need a slow fire and a heavy pot to render the lard. Put ¼" of water in the pot to keep the fat from scorching at first. Remove anything that is not fat. Cut into very small pieces. Put a small layer of fat in the pot. When the first layer of fat has started to melt, add more. Do not fill the kettle to the top -- it can boil over too easily. Stir frequently and keep fire low.

The temperature of the lard will be 212°F at first, but as the water evaporates, the temperature will rise. This will take a long time at low heat and you must stir the lard frequently to prevent scorching. As the lard renders, the cracklings will float to the surface. When the lard is almost done and the cracklings have lost the rest of their moisture, they will sink to the bottom. Turn off the heat and allow the lard to settle and cool slightly. Then carefully strain the liquid and cracklings through a cheese cloth and into clean containers.

Fill containers to the top -- the lard will contract while cooling. Chill as quickly as possible for a fine-grained shortening. Air, light, and moisture can make lard rancid and sour. After it has been thoroughly cooled, cover the containers tightly and store in a dark, cool area.

Render any type of fat using the same method.

How to Make
Pemmican

Pemmican is a Native American Indian survival food that requires no refrigeration or canning and has a very long shelf life. It is similar to a homemade Granola Bar. It is a compact energy source that contains protein, fat, carbohydrates, fiber, natural fruit sugars, vitamins, and minerals. It is a simple combination of lean meat jerky, fat and dried fruit.

It can easily be made in the wilderness without any special cookware or equipment. The following recipe uses equal amounts of dried lean meat, dried fruit, and melted fat. Pemmican is a very flexible food. Vary the quantities of these three basic ingredients to more fully utilize the food you have available, but only use just enough melted fat to hold your pemmican together. If you have more lean meat and/or more dried fruit than you can use, then you can simply convert the extra lean meat into meat jerky and store the dried fruit for winter. Depending on the summer fruit and berries available, you could use more or less dried fruit or berries in the recipe.

During the summer when wild game and berries are widely available you can harvest as much as you can and then process it all into pemmican for winter consumption when little or no food will be available. This is the reason pemmican was such an important survival food for the Native American Indians.

Basic Ingredients:
- 1 Cup of Dried Meat
- 1 Cup of Dried Fruit or Berries
- 1 Cup of Melted Animal Fat

Dry the meat. Use deer, moose, caribou, or beef, but not pork. It takes between one to two pounds of fresh meat to make one cup of dried meat. See 'How to Make Jerky'. If the meat jerky bends it still contains too much moisture. If it crumbles it is too dry but it can still be used. Grind the dried meat into a course powder.
Use one or two types of fruit or berries, such as blueberries, huckleberries, currants, raisins, apples, apricots, or cherries. Cut the fruit into thin slices or pieces and allow them to dry in the sun. Dry them in the oven at the same time you dry your meat jerky. An electric food dehydrator will also work, if electricity is available. Grind the dried fruit into a powder. You can leave little lumps to provide texture and taste.

Mix the dried meat powder and the dried fruit powder together in a bowl. You can then add salt into the mixture to enhance its flavor at this time. Salt will also increase the shelf life of the pemmican as it helps to retard the future growth of harmful microorganisms. The salt will *not* kill those microorganisms but it will help to keep them from multiplying. If you do not have any salt then you should keep your pemmican in a sealed glass jar, plastic storage container or plastic freezer bag

Change it up by adding a little honey or some minced dried onion for flavor. Or add a few crushed nuts. However, nuts contain oil and the nuts will shorten the shelf life of your pemmican. When adding these optional ingredients you should begin with a very small batch of pemmican. This will permit you to experiment and determine if the results are agreeable.

Use fresh beef fat or pork fat or bear fat. Animal fat will quickly become rancid and it should be rendered as soon as possible. See 'How to Render Lard'. When the fat is completely melted, gradually pour it over the meat-fruit mixture in the bowl. Stir until the mixture is well coated and sticks together. Then spread it out like dough, allow it to cool completely then cut it to 1 inch wide by 4 inch long pieces.

Pemmican does not need to be wrapped for short term storage. Place the pemmican in plastic zip lock bags or in plastic storage containers with a tight fitting lid and can be stored safely for 8 months. By keeping the temperature between 40 to 75 degrees Fahrenheit (4 to 24 degrees Celsius) pemmican can be stored for several years.

How to Make a
Solar Box Oven

This is a great solar oven design that can be built quickly from two cardboard boxes. After your solar oven is made, you may cook *anything* that needs a temperature of up to 325 degree F. If the food needs a hotter temperature extend the cooking time. You can bake bread, pies, meat or just about anything you use an oven for, the solar box oven will bake using the power of the sun.

Solar Oven Design Materials

- Two cardboard boxes, with an inner box that is at least 15" x 15" (38cm x 38cm), but bigger is better
- The outer box should be larger all around, but it doesn't matter how much bigger, as long as there is a half inch (1.5cm) or more of airspace between the two boxes and the distance between the two boxes does not have to be equal all the way around. It is easy to adjust the size of a cardboard box by cutting and gluing it
- One sheet of cardboard to make the lid, which must be approximately 2" - 3" (4 - 8cm) larger all the way around than the top of the finished cooker
- One small roll of aluminum foil
- One can of non-toxic flat-black spray paint or one small jar of black tempera paint
- At least 8 ounces of white glue
- One Reynolds Oven Cooking Bag®. They are rated for 400° F (204.4° C). They are not UV resistant so they will become brittle and opaque over time and may need to be replaced. A sheet of glass can also be used

Building the Base

- Fold the top flaps closed on the outer box and set the inner box on top and trace a line around it onto the top of the outer box
- Remove the inner box and cut along this line to form a hole in the top of the outer box
- Decide how deep you want your oven to be about 1" or 2.5cm bigger than your largest pot and at least 1" shorter than the outer box
- Slit the corners of the inner box with a knife down to that height

- Fold each side down forming extended flaps. Folding is smoother if you first draw a firm line from the end of one cut to the other where the folds are to go
- Glue aluminum foil to the inside of both boxes and also to the inside of the remaining top flaps of the outer box. Don't waste your time being neat on the outer box, since it will never be seen, nor will it experience any wear. The inner box will be visible even after assembly
- Glue the top flaps closed on the outer box
- Place some wads of crumpled newspaper into the outer box
- Set the inner box down inside the hole in the outer box, the flaps on the inner box just touch the top of the outer box (Figure 3)
- Glue these flaps onto the top of the outer box. Trim the excess flap length to be even with the perimeter of the outer box
- Finally, to make the drip pan, cut a piece of cardboard, the same size as the bottom of the interior of the oven and apply foil to one side
- Paint this foiled side black and allow it to dry. Put this in the oven (black side up) and place your pots on it when cooking. The base is now finished

Building the Removable Lid
- Take the large sheet of cardboard and lay it on top of the base. Trace its outline then cut and fold down the edges to form a lip of about 3" (7.5cm)
- Fold the corner flaps around and glue to the side lid flaps
- Orient the corrugations so that they go from left to right as you face the oven so that later the prop may be inserted into the corrugations

- One trick you can use to make the lid fit well is to lay the pencil or pen against the side of the box when marking. Don't glue this lid to the box; you'll need to remove it to move pots in and out of the oven
- To make the reflector flap, draw a line on the lid, forming a rectangle the same size as the oven opening
- Cut around three sides and fold the resulting flap up forming the reflector. Foil this flap on the inside
- To make a prop bend a 12" (30cm) piece of hanger wire
- Next, turn the lid upside-down and glue the oven bag in place. We have had great success using the turkey size oven bag (19" x 23 1/2", 47.5cm x 58.5cm) applied as is, i.e., without opening it up. This makes a double layer of plastic.
- The two layers are separated from each other to form airspace as the oven cooks
- When using this method, it is important to also glue the bag closed on its open end. This stops water vapor from entering the bag and condensing
- Alternately you can cut any size oven bag open to form a flat sheet large enough to cover the oven opening

How to Make a
Sourdough Starter

On the cattle drive the starter was prized by both cook and cowboy. It was not uncommon on cool nights for the trail cook to wrap the barrel in a blanket and tuck it into his bed using his body heat to keep the precious batter warm.

To keep it fermenting, the batter had to be replenished and kept warm. At a ranch house, the task was relatively easy. The starter was kept warm by storing it behind a constantly stoked stove.

A good sourdough starter can last for years, passed down from generation to generation with the proper care. The sourdough starters were originally produced by wild yeasts and a flour and water mixture that is used to raise the bread.

There are many variations to making a sourdough starter. Here is an easy sourdough starter recipe:

- 2 cups flour
- 1 tbsp. Sugar (optional)
- 1 package active dry yeast
- 2 cups warm water (105 ° - 115° F)

Combine the flour, sugar, and dry yeast in a large glass or ceramic bowl. Gradually add the warm water to the dry ingredients, beating until smooth. Cover with cheesecloth and let stand in a warm place for four to six days.

When mixture is bubbly and has a pleasant sour smell, it is ready to use. If mixture has a strange color tinge to it, discard it and start over. Keep it in the refrigerator, covered until ready to bake.

After you use the sourdough starter, replace with equal amounts of flour and water mixture along with a pinch of sugar. So, if you remove 1 cup starter, replace with 1 cup water *and* 1 cup flour. Mix until smooth, cover and leave out on the counter in a warm place until mixture bubbles well, at least eight hours. Store loosely covered in the refrigerator. If a clear to light brown liquid has accumulated on top, don't worry, this is an alcohol base liquid that occurs with fermentation. Just stir this back into the starter, the alcohol bakes off and that wonderful sourdough flavor remains. Use and replenish at least once every two weeks.

How to Grow
Sprouts

Growing your own sprouts is very easy and can save yourself a lot of money. Sprouting at home takes only a few minutes a day, and can produce a good part of your daily requirements of the nutrients you need from fresh produce. The hassles are minor, the costs are low, and the freshness is wonderful. Nothing beats local produce, and you can't get much more "local" than to grow sprouts in your own kitchen.

When purchasing seeds for sprouting, be certain that the seeds are intended for food and not for planting. This precaution is necessary because some seeds meant for planting have been treated with fungicides or insecticides.

You will need a mason jar with a screw-on ring as part of the lid which will hold your screen in place. Muslin, cheesecloth, nylon or wire mesh is placed over the top of the jar allowing the seeds air and to be rinsed and drained. You should always use the widest mesh you can without the small seeds falling through. Wider mesh allows rinsing and draining more easily and improves air-flow as well.

Decide which seed you are going to sprout then:
- Put about 1 tablespoon of small seeds or 4 tablespoons of beans or large seeds
- Soak the seeds by filling the jar with water and leave to soak for 8 - 12 hours or for the time noted for the seed you are sprouting
- Drain the water out of the jar and rinse; fill jar with cool water and twirl the seeds around
- Pour water off and repeat once or twice more

This is the hardest part of sprouting; once done rinsing you need to get as much of the water out of the jar as possible.

- Turn the jar screen down and gently shake it up and down over and over and over again until no more water comes out. Shake more than you think is necessary
- Keep the jar upside down or at an angle - Remember to drain any excess water because the sprouts should not stand in water as they will rot and spoil
- Place the jar in very low light for the first few days; never put a jar in direct sunlight
- To keep the sprouts constantly damp, repeat the rinsing 2-3 times a day

- When the seeds/beans begin to sprout - usually about the fourth day - move the jar to a brighter place to activate the chlorophyll and turn the sprouts green. Very little sunlight is needed to turn the sprouts green

Sprouts from beans, peas, etc., are ready earlier and can be eaten when they are 3-6 days old. Sprouts need to be stored in the refrigerator once they are ready to eat. Put the sprouts in tightly sealed bags, and they will remain flavorful and crisp for one to two weeks. Rinsing the sprouts daily under cold water can extend their life.

Alfalfa, Broccoli, Clover, and Radish - should be soaked for 6-12 hours. 1-part seed gives 10-parts sprouts in approximately 5-6 days. Sprouts can be eaten after 3 days. When the root is 1-2 inches long, it will begin to develop tiny green leaves. At this stage, it needs to be eaten immediately so the plant will not switch to photosynthesis that exhausts the stored food in the seed.

Peas - when soaked in a glass jar, will grow sprouts in about 3 days. When the roots are 2-inches long, they are ready to eat. 1-part peas give 2-parts sprouts.

Lentils - can be grown in either a glass jar or a plant pot and need to be soaked for 12-hours. *Rinse* lentils 'til the water runs clear, or you won't get your sprouts out of the jar without a chisel. The sprouts are ready in 3-4 days. Lentil sprouts are ready to be eaten when the root is 1-inch long. 1-part lentils give 6-parts sprouts.

Barley, Oats, Rye, and Wheat - should be soaked for 12-hours and then can either be grown as "grass" to harvest, or sprouts ready to eat after 3-4 days. The ideal length for eating is about 1/2-inch. 1-part seed gives 2-parts sprouts.

Soybeans - you can grow these sprouts in a glass jar or a pot. They need to be soaked for 12-hours and sprouts are usually ready after 3-5 days. They are ready to eat when the root is 2-inches long. 1-part beans give 4-parts sprouts.

Mung Beans - Soaking for 12-hours, usually are ready to eat after 3-5 days, when the bright white root grows from 1-2 inches long. 1-part beans give 4-parts sprouts. You can't grow big thick mungs in a jar unless you want to break the Jar when they're done - that's the only way you'll get the sprouts out. Grow the sweet and tiny mungs when using a jar.

Sunflower - Sprout hulled (de-shelled) sunflower seeds in a jar. For sunflower greens, soak and plant the small black sunflower seeds (hull intact) and grow them like cereal grasses in a tray. Give it a try and experiment with different seeds and their flavors. Also experiment with growing grass and cereal seeds for something new.

How to Make

Whey

Yogurt, kefir and buttermilk are all common probiotic foods. These are all fermented dairy products that are eaten while the bacteria are still alive. Whey is the liquid remaining after milk has been curdled and then strained. Whey is also the starter for lacto-fermented fruits, vegetables, and beverages.

Put plain yogurt in a dish towel or cheese cloth and let the whey drip out into a mason jar overnight. Once the whey is separated, delicious cream cheese is what is left in the cheesecloth. Refrigerated whey will last for months.

Make fresh cottage cheese by adding lemon juice or vinegar to fresh milk, let it sit for ten minutes then strain. This will leave cottage cheese. But if you stir the mixture together and do not strain, this makes buttermilk.

How to Make
Yogurt

Yogurt is very easy to make. You will need fresh milk; cow, goat or soy, pasteurized or unpasteurized, whole, 2% or non-fat all work. Also you will need a thermometer that ranges from the 100° up past 180°, a jar and a way to keep the yogurt warm. Some people use a heating pad or if you have a gas stove with a pilot light, this will keep the interior of the oven at around 80 to 100 degrees, which is perfect for the yogurt.

The amount of milk used will be the amount of yogurt you will get. Ready the jar and lid by thoroughly washing. It is best to use a double boiler or water jacket but not necessary. In a large saucepan heat the milk over medium low heat until it reaches 180°. This kills off any competing bacteria so that the yogurt will respond better to the acidophilus cultures. Remove from the heat and allow the milk to cool to 110° to 115°. If the milk is any hotter than this then it will kill off the yogurt cultures.

Add a few teaspoons of store-bought plain yogurt to the warm milk. Stir well. Allow it sit for a few minutes and stir a final time.

Carefully pour the mixture into a very clean, quart-sized container.

Incubate the yogurt in a warm spot for 6 to 8 hours, or until it is set almost as thick as store-bought yogurt. Chill and eat.

Add your own recipes here...

"We will always remember. We will always be proud. We will always be prepared, so we will always be free"
– Ronald Reagan

Chapter Nine

Natural and Man-Made Emergencies and Disasters

Located along the edge of the tectonic plates is the "Ring of Fire", known for its very active earthquakes and volcanoes. But there are active fault lines all over North America and the world. Most were presumed inactive because there has been no activity; until recently. The 5.8 magnitude 2011 earthquake in New York was a shock to the people on the east coast. The earth shook; some people panicked and wondered what was happening. If the earthquake would have happened in California, everyone would have known exactly what was happening. New Yorkers are used to blizzards not earthquakes and some Californians have never even seen snow.

The natural events that are common to the area have warning systems in place. Natives born in the area are taught what to do next; but it is the un-common events that will be a great surprise.

"Do what you can, with what you have, where you are."
— Theodore Roosevelt

If you travel, research what natural disasters are common to that area. What farfetched disaster could, maybe, possibly happen? A tornado in Maine, a blizzard in LA, Terrorist EMP attack, a solar flare that rips the electromagnetic field from the earth, a nuclear meltdown in Chicago or a super-volcano that blankets ash eight feet high across two thirds of the United States?; all possible, maybe not probable, but then again, why not?

Disasters and emergencies can happen with or without notice. But as with all emergencies, being aware and knowledgeable will get you a lot further than those that do not heed the warnings.

The type of emergency or disaster will dictate how you prepare and how you will actually handle the situation. Some little event can be solved in a very short amount of time, while other emergencies or disaster need to be addressed by a large group of people, charities and government agencies. While there are events that can be avoided by taking precautions there are also the man-made events that will happen without our consent and without warning.

Still, we need to be aware of any and every kind of event that could happen; natural or man-made.

A few disasters will have overlapping problems. For example terrorist and biological and chemical warfare, earthquake and fires, Nuclear with EMP or Solar flare and EMP. Use all the information to get through the difficult events. Stay calm and do NOT panic. That is the one way to cause you and your family hardship and heartache. Be prepared and you will be OK.

Emergency and Disaster Type List

- Earthquake
- Fire
- Floods
- Hurricane
- Tornadoes
- Wildfire
- Volcanoes
- Terrorist Threat and Attack
- Chemical and Biological
- Nuclear Disaster
- Epidemic and Pandemic
- Magnetic Reversal and Solar Flare
- Electromagnetic Pulse (EMP)
- Looters
- Alien Invasion

Let Your Family Know You're Safe

If your community experiences a disaster, you can register on the American Red Cross Safe and Well Web site at RedCross.org. This helps keep your family aware of your whereabouts and to let them know you are safe.

If you don't have Internet access, call 1-866-GET-INFO to register yourself and your family.

Earthquake

An earthquake is a sudden snap of the tectonic plates that push against each other beneath the earth's surface causing a rapid shaking of the earth. Earthquakes strike suddenly and without warning. They can occur at any time of the year, day or night. Prepping for an earthquake is easier than having to deal with the potential harm that may occur if you do not have the basic knowledge of what to do. Whether it is a big or small earthquake; prepping can save your life.

- Keep your emergency/disaster kit in an easy-to-access location.
- Keep a flashlight with fully charged batteries by each family member's bed
- Learn how to shut off the gas valves in your home and keep a wrench close by
- Bolt and brace water heaters, gas appliances, bookcases, china cabinets and other tall furniture to wall studs
- Install strong latches on cabinets
- Know the fire evacuation and earthquake plans for all of the buildings you occupy regularly
- Do not hang heavy items such as pictures or mirrors over beds, couches or anywhere people sleep or sit.
- Pick safe places in each room of your home and workplace, away from windows
- Practice -- cover and hold on. If you do not have sturdy furniture to hold on to, sit on the floor next to an interior wall and cover your head and neck with your arms.

Once the quake starts:

- Doorways are no stronger than any other part of the structure. During an earthquake, get under a sturdy piece of furniture.
- If you are in bed when the quake starts, move to the floor at the end or side of your bed, whichever is away from a window, curl up and hold on. Protect your head with a pillow if you can.

If you are outside when the quake starts:

- Find a clear spot away from buildings, power lines, trees, streetlights, drop to the ground and stay there until the shaking stops
- If you are in your car, pull over to a clear location, avoid bridges, overpasses and power lines, stay inside keeping your seatbelt fastened

When the quake stops

- Avoid bridges and ramps that may have been damaged.
- Stay out of damaged buildings
- Listen to a portable, battery-operated or hand-crank radio for updates
- Check yourself for injuries and get first aid, if necessary, before helping others

When all is said and done, there may be intense aftershocks. Treat the aftershocks as you did the first earthquake. Landslides or even a tsunami are often generated by earthquakes, so be keenly aware of the situation and any hazards that may be present.

If an earthquake happens out at sea you may not be aware of the dangers that are associated with the tsunami that may come.

Native residents usually are taught the dangers of their low lying community being in harm's way if a tsunami or tidal wave were to hit. If the sea water recesses a great distance for what looks like low tide may be the first sign of a tsunami coming. Instructions are to get to high ground as quickly as possible.

Fire

Home fires are one of the leading causes of personal emergencies in the home. Would you know what to do if a fire started in your home? Would your kids know what to do? Take the time now to review fire safety facts and tips so your family will be prepared in the event of a fire emergency in your home.

Fire Prevention
The best way to practice fire safety is to make sure a fire doesn't break out in the first place. That means you should always be aware of potential hazards in your home. Start by keeping these tips in mind:
- Electrical appliances in good condition - without loose or frayed cords or plugs
- Outlets not overloaded with plugs from the TV, computer, printer, video game system and stereo
- Light fixtures use the correct wattage bulbs
- Don't run electrical wires under rugs
- Lamps and night-lights are not touching bedspreads, drapes or any fabrics.

The leading kitchen fire causes are food left unsupervised on a stove, in an oven or microwave, grease spills, a dish towel too close to the burner, a toaster or toaster oven flare-up, etc. Do not wear loose-fitting clothing while cooking that could catch fire around the stove. Simply be aware of the situation and keep your wits about you while you are in the kitchen.

Fireplaces should be kept clean and covered with a screen to keep sparks from jumping out. Only wood should be burned in the fireplace. Also, have the chimney professionally cleaned once a year.

It's a fact that having a smoke alarm in the house cuts your risk of dying in a fire *in half.* Almost 60% of all fatal residential fires occur in homes that don't have smoke alarms, so this may be the single most important thing you can do to keep your family safe from fires. If your home doesn't have smoke or carbon monoxide alarms, now is the time to install them on every level of your home and in each bedroom. If possible, choose one with a 10-year lithium battery.

Because smoke rises, smoke detectors should always be placed on ceilings or high on walls. If a smoke detector near the kitchen goes off while you're cooking, *do not* take the battery out of it — you may forget to replace it. Open the doors and windows instead. Or you might consider installing a rate-of-rise heat detector for places like the kitchen, where smoke or steam from cooking are likely to cause false alarms. These alarms can sense when the temperature reaches a set critical point or when it rises by more than a certain number of degrees a minute.

Fire Extinguishers
Have fire extinguishers strategically placed around your house — at least one on each floor and in the kitchen; this one should be an all-purpose extinguisher, meaning it can be used on grease and electrical fires, the basement, the garage, or workshop

area. Keep them out of reach of children. Fire extinguishers are best used when a fire is contained in a small area and after the fire department has already been called. To use an extinguisher:

- Pull the pin
- Release the lock with the nozzle pointing away from you.
- Aim low; Point the extinguisher at the base of the fire.
- Squeeze the lever slowly and evenly.
- Sweep the nozzle from side to side.

The best time to learn how to use the fire extinguisher is *now*, before you ever need it. Fire extinguishers have gauges on them indicating when they need to be replaced and should be checked regularly to make sure they are still functional.

Floods

Floods are caused by rising water in an existing waterway, such as a river, stream, or drainage ditch that overflow into a normally dry area. Flooding is a longer term event as where a flash flood happens within a few minutes to a couple hours after a large quantity of rain falls within a short amount of time.

The best way to prevent damage from flooding in your home is to move away from the flood plain area before one occurs. Unless you have to live in the area, choose the highest area possible. If you learned anything in the last decade, it would be floods can and do occur in low-lying areas previously thought safe. Rivers and streams rise to record levels, levy's break, and too much concrete near cities and towns make it so the ground cannot absorb all that rain.

When the water starts to spill over the banks of a river close to home, sand bags and attempts to re-route the water are ways to help lessen the potential damage the water will do to your home.

Flash floods are usually characterized by raging torrents after heavy rains that rip through river beds, mountain canyons or urban streets. They can occur within minutes or a few hours of excessive rainfall. They can also occur after a levee or dam has failed, or after a sudden release of water by a debris or ice dam.

While driving, exercise caution when crossing over water flowing on the road; it doesn't take much water to float a car or truck. If you're stuck in a flood, follow your instincts and move to the highest ground possible.

If you have flood insurance, check the wording to make sure it covers natural flooding from waterway over flow along with pipe breaks inside your home.

Hurricane

A hurricane is a type of thunderstorm and a counter-clockwise circulation of winds near the earth's surface; the generic term for a low pressure system that generally forms in the tropics. The hurricane season lasts from June to November, with the peak season from mid-August to late October.

Hurricanes can create storm surges along the coast, spawn tornadoes and micro-bursts; winds can exceed

155 miles per hour; cause catastrophic damage to coastlines and several hundred miles inland. Hurricanes are classified into five categories based on their wind speed, central pressure, and damage potential.

The best thing you should do, of course, is to evacuate as soon as the warning is heard. Follow the evacuation and grab list. Board up the house, shut off the water main valve, electricity and gas and leave before the roads get packed.

Tornadoes

Although tornadoes occur in many parts of the world, these twisting destructive forces of nature are found most frequently in the United States, east of the Rocky Mountains, during the spring and summer months. In an average year, 800 tornadoes are reported nationwide, resulting in injuries and deaths. A tornado is defined as a violently rotating column of air extending from a thunderstorm to the ground. The most violent tornadoes are capable of tremendous destruction with wind speeds of 250 mph or more. Flying debris from tornadoes causes most deaths and injuries.

Weather Service personnel use information from weather radar, spotters, and other sources to issue severe thunderstorm and tornado *warning* for areas where severe weather is imminent. When conditions are favourable for severe weather to develop, a severe thunderstorm or tornado *watch* is issued. Severe thunderstorm warnings are passed to local radio and television stations and are broadcast over local NOAA Weather Radio stations serving the warned areas. These warnings are also relayed to local emergency management and public safety officials who can activate the community's warning system.

It was thought that if you live near rivers, lakes and mountains you are safe from tornadoes but the truth is no terrain is safe from tornadoes. In the late 1980's, a tornado swept through Yellowstone National Park leaving a path of destruction up and down a 10,000 ft. mountain

The myth that windows should be opened before a tornado approaches to equalize the low pressure which would causes the buildings to "explode" is also not true; by opening your windows, wind enters the structure allowing damage that may not have occurred if the windows were left closed; instead, immediately go to a basement, interior room, or bathroom without windows to insure you are safe from broken glass.

Each year, many people are killed or seriously injured by tornadoes despite advance warning. Some did not hear the warning while others who heard it chose not to believe the tornado would actually affect them. When the warning is issued and received, it is up to you to act upon the threat and seek shelter as soon as possible, implement your family disaster plan and take the emergency/disaster disaster bags or kits with you.

Wildfire

There are over two thousand wildfires per year per state in the US, 98 percent of wildfires are contained at less than 100 acres and 17 percent of wildfires are caused by lightning. While some wildfires threaten homes and commercial buildings, there are ways to protect yourself and your home.   Prepare your property if you live in a high-risk area. Thousands of homes are evacuated every year; families can make the transition much easier by implementing an evacuation plan.

Wildfire Preparedness Check List
The more "yes" answers you have, the more you are prepared in the event of a wildfire threat.

Your Home
- ❑ Fire-resistant roof i.e. metal, tile, composition?
- ❑ Non-flammable siding materials?
- ❑ Roof and gutters free from leaves and needles?
- ❑ Wooden deck facing or overhanging level ground?
- ❑ Large glass windows, facing level ground?
- ❑ Deck, porch, vents or house screened to keep sparks out?
- ❑ Chimney extending above the roofline and spark arrester in place?
- ❑ Signs and address are well marked and visible both night and day?
- ❑ Roads wide and accommodating into and out of your area for easy access by emergency vehicles

Around the House
- ❑ Firewood and other burnable items 30 – 100 ft from house?
- ❑ Clear of weeds, tall grasses and brush?
- ❑ Debris cleared and trees pruned 10 ft up from base of trunk?
- ❑ Tree limbs pruned at least 10 ft from roof or 15 ft laterally from chimney?
- ❑ Store all gas, oil, propane tanks and other chemicals away from the house?

Water Supply
- ❏ Pressurized hydrants or dry hydrants available?
- ❏ Water sources such as ponds or streams accessible?
- ❏ Power lines buried and not susceptible to fire?
- ❏ Well pumps maintained with uninterrupted electricity?

Volcanoes

Active volcanoes in the United States exist in Hawaii, Alaska and the Pacific Northwest. But throughout history there have been instances where volcanoes pop up in places that previously had no activity. A farmer in South America ploughed his field and the next day there was a mountain of dirt that pushed up over night.

When pressure builds up within a volcano, the molten rock has the potential to erupt. The eruption sends forth lava, poisonous gases and ash that can sometimes travel hundreds of miles, usually downwind.

If you live near a potentially active volcano look up and/or research the instructions of local emergency officials; knowing your community's warning systems and disaster plans, including evacuation routes will help you evacuate quickly. Have your Emergency Car Kit, 72 hour Kit and Emergency Binder ready. Plan ahead by adding goggles and something to cover your nose and mouth for every member of your family to your emergency/disaster kit.

If you are unable to evacuate you should remain indoors, seal the doors, windows and ventilation airways with duct tape until the ash settles. Stay informed; listen to your local authorities on what you should do next.

A large volcanic area called a caldera can be considered a super-volcano when the amount of more than 20% of its molten reservoir in cubic meters of rock is expelled upon eruption. There are eight such calderas located around the world.

The Yellowstone caldera, approximately 35 miles by 45 miles across erupted 650,000 years ago and before that, 1.2 million years ago. This pattern would put it today at 50,000 years overdue for an eruption.

Researchers report the super-volcano underneath the state of Wyoming has been rising at a record rate since 2004. Its floor has gone up three inches per year for the last three years indicating the fastest rate since records began in 1923.

Geologist state it is a real possibility that it could blow at any time. But, as with any kind of natural event, scientist can only go off of the information that presents itself prior to the event, estimating the possibilities and probabilities of best and worst case scenarios. It may or may not happen in our lifetime. Or it may develop over the next few days and happen within a week. No one truly knows when it will happen.

Terrorist Threat and Attack

A growing concern among Homeland Security professionals is that terrorists will someday unleash chemical, biological or radiological materials. These weapons have been used very little so far. Where terrorists have tried to carry out attacks, they have generally used relatively simple materials; the impact of any attack would depend heavily on the chemical or biological type and the chosen method of dissemination or the weather conditions at the time. With terrorist attacks, you will not receive prior warning and the exact nature of an incident may not be immediately obvious.

With the unprecedented terrorist attack from an extreme religious group on 9/11, we have changed the airport and transportation security. The attack brought on the addition of Homeland security which has stopped countless terrorist attempts that we may never know about.

In 2001, the U.S. government established a commission to assess the threat to the United States from Electromagnetic Pulse (EMP) attack. Such an attack would involve the detonation of a nuclear warhead at high altitude over the American mainland, producing a shockwave powerful enough to knock out electrical power, electronics, communications and transportation, sewage systems, refrigeration, water-pumping stations and anything that relies on electricity and is not hardened with a faraday cage would be affected or completely destroyed. We at this time have no stand-by replacement parts or plan for recovery of such a large attack.

The EMP commission also reported that Iran — which is feverishly working to acquire nuclear weapons, has conducted tests in which it launched missiles and exploded warheads at high altitudes. The CIA has translated Iranian military journals in which EMP attacks against the U.S. are explicitly discussed.

The development of electromagnetic pulse technology has made it possible for a rouge terror organization to harness an E-Bomb for less than $400. The physics behind such a weapons use as well as the overwhelming hatred of freedom by extremist is a terrifying, yet very plausible reality.

Chemical & Biological

An act of biological or chemical terrorism might range from dissemination of aerosolized anthrax spores to food product contamination. Any attack would be localized. The possibility of biological or chemical terrorism is very real in light of events during the past 10+ years such as the Saran gas attack in the Tokyo subway and the discovery of military bio-weapons programs in Iraq and the former Soviet Union.

Predicting when and how such an attack might occur is not possible, but treating any ill affect can be handled the same as with an epidemic or severe cases of illness. The homeland security, CIA and FBI would investigate.

The public health infrastructure became more prepared to prevent illness and injury that would result from biological and chemical terrorism by participated in developing a strategic plan with the combined efforts of these offices:

- Center for Disease Control
- Epidemiology Program Office,
- National Institute for Occupational Safety and Health,
- Office of Health and Safety,
- Public Health Practice Program Office,
- National Center for Infectious Diseases,
- National Center for Environmental Health,
- National Immunization Program, and
- National Center for Injury Prevention and Control

As with emerging infectious diseases, early detection and control of biological or chemical attacks depends on the rapid mobilization of public health workers, emergency responders, and private health-care providers. Large-scale outbreaks will also require rapid development and distribution of large quantities of drugs and vaccines.

Viral Hemorrhagic Fever
VHFs refer to a group of illnesses that are caused by several distinct families of viruses. In general, the term "viral hemorrhagic fever" is used to describe a severe multi-system syndrome, where multiple organ systems in the body are affected. VHFs include four families of viruses: Filiviruses such as the Ebola and Marburg viruses, Arena viruses such as Lassa, bunya virus (Rift Valley Fever) and Flaviviruses such as yellow fever and dengue. They can all cause life-threatening illnesses. Some, including Ebola, Marburg and Lassa, are contagious. Fatality rate is about 90 percent for Ebola and 1 percent for Lassa.

VHFs are not expected to become a bio-weapon of choice since people die quickly from them and thus do not get a chance to infect others.

VHFs naturally occur in humans only after contact with an infected insect, rodent or larger mammal. Transmission can happen through touching fecal matter, receiving an insect bite or handling contaminated meat. It is possible VHFs can be manufactured for aerosol dissemination but the bacterium does not flourish well in this form.

Once a person becomes infected with VHF, the overall vascular system becomes damaged and the body's ability to regulate itself is impaired. The symptoms are often accompanied by bleeding; however, the bleeding is rarely life-threatening.

Some types of VHF's can cause mild illnesses, while in severe cases the internal and external bleeding in internal organs, under the skin and from the eyes, nose, mouth and ears can be life-threatening. The symptoms generally include high fever, dizziness, muscle aches and exhaustion which may be felt from two days to three weeks after exposure. If left untreated the advanced symptoms include shock, seizures and coma.

Treatment is available for some VHFs, but not all. A yellow fever vaccine is available but no treatments or vaccines exist for Ebola or Marburg. Patient care can be taken to prevent shock and help the organs to continue to function.

Marburg and Ebola are hard to acquire from the wild because their natural host is unknown and outbreaks are rare. VHFs are studied in high-security labs. Research on Ebola and several others was done by the Soviet Union before its bio-warfare program was dismantled, but experts warn the microbe collections in Russia, Kazakhstan, Georgia and Uzbekistan are not adequately secured and terrorist groups might be able to obtain these strains of plague, tularemia and VHFs.

Nuclear Disaster
What to Do Before, During and After

There are numerous ways that a nuclear disaster could happen; whether it is from a terrorist attack, war with nuclear weapons or a nuclear meltdown. Threats to our liberty are constantly changing as the world changes. Iran is currently working on a nuclear program that many people fear will lead to nuclear weapons. North Korea's has a growing nuclear arsenal, misplaced old Soviet Union weapons are sold on the black market which could be made available to extremist or the One World Order organization want so desperately to control people they may just go nuclear to make sure it happens; whatever the reasons a nuclear event may come up, you will need to be aware and ready for the multiple facets of a nuclear event.

If you live in a dangerous target area, your hometown will most likely get hit. A one megaton nuclear device is not as strong as a 25MT so the radiation will not be as strong in the smaller size.

Never look directly at the explosion, it will blind you. The light or flash can be seen up to 50 miles away. The immediate area is destroyed from one to sixteen miles across.

The blast creates a debris mushroom cloud and the wind created by the upward push of air can reach 200 miles per hour.

The radioactive fallout is the particulate matter (dust) produced by the pulverized concrete buildings and dirt. This material is then carried high up into the air. Most of it settles back to earth downwind of the explosion. The heaviest, most dangerous, and most noticeable fallout, will fall closer to ground zero, minutes after an explosion. The smaller and lighter dust-like particles will be arriving hours later, as they drift much farther downwind, often for hundreds of miles. Once it *arrives*, visible or not, all that will fall will have done so usually in an hour's time.

This radioactive fallout emits penetrating radiation energy; similar to x-ray's. This radiation, not the fallout dust, can go through walls, roofs and protective clothing. Even if you manage not to inhale or ingest the dust, and keep it off your skin, hair, and clothes, the radiation penetrating your home is extremely dangerous.

Radioactive fallout kills and is not perceptible to the human senses. It gives off so much energy its intensity is quickly lost. For example, fallout emitting gamma ray radiation at a rate over 500 R/hr (fatal with one hour of exposure) shortly after an explosion, weakens to only 1/10th as strong 7 hours later. Two days later, it's only 1/100th as strong as it was initially. Under normal circumstances the radioactive decays or dies down in about 14 -21 days.

With a nuclear plant meltdown, the *radiations* main source is so large, the decay of radiation is not within days but takes years, and even decades to eventual weaken and clear.

What to Do *Before* the Disaster Happens

To protect yourself from the radiation and fallout, you need a fallout shelter. If you live at or near a place that could be ground zero, you are better off with a blast shelter.

Blast shelters are usually buried deeper than fallout shelters, have hardened doors, blast valves and are designed to withstand the over pressure and negative pressure associated with a nuclear blast. For most of us, however, a fallout shelter will do.

Fallout shelters rely on earth, sand, cement, brick, cement block or other dense material to block the radiation until it lessens. What stops radiation, and thus shields your family, is simply putting mass between them and the radiation source. Like police body armour stopping bullets, mass stops (absorbs) radiation. The thicker and heavier the mass, with every inch more of mass you add, the more radiation it stops.

The goals of your family fallout shelter are: to place sufficient mass between you and the fallout radiation, have the food, water and sanitation ready and lastly to make the shelter as tolerable as possible while the radiation slowly subsides.

If you do not have a ready-made shelter available you can make an expedient shelter in the basement. People *can* survive a nuclear event if they get into a proper shelter to safely wait out the dangers; becoming less dangerous with every passing hour.

You can find minimal protection in a full basement of a residential home. A basement fallout shelter can be set up prior to an emergency and without too much hassle. Some of the advantages to a basement shelter besides the fact you can enter and exit your shelter without leaving your home are:

- You can overpressure the entire basement; route the air outflow pipe into the adjacent basement area and achieve overpressure protection for the entire basement.
- This allows you to store items out there and retrieve them without worrying about what you are breathing.
- You probably already have electricity, water, and sewer in your basement.
- This will save time and money when putting together your shelter.
- By installing a battery capable air filter, you will assure continuous overpressure for many hours after a power outage.
- By using the basement you can easily place a blast door into the side of your shelter. This will make it easier to enter the shelter then having to lower supplies, people, and pets down through a blast hatch and down a ladder.
- Any radioactive fallout that lands on your roof will be about 10 feet from the top of your shelter; since mass, time and distance are the only things that protect us, this is beneficial.
- There are many other uses for your shelter: a vault for your valuables, a panic room in case of a home invasion robbery, can be used as a communications center and/or a food storage area.

For an expedient *last-minute* basement shelter, push a heavy table into the corner that has the highest ground level soil outside; ideally needs to be above the top of the table shelter inside. If no heavy table is available, you can take internal doors off their hinges and lay them on supports to create your table top roof. Then pile any available mass on top and around the other two open sides such as books, bricks, sandbags, heavy appliances, full file cabinets, full water containers, your food stock, even boxes and pillow cases full of anything heavy. Everything you can pile up and around that has mass will help absorb and stop more radiation from penetrating inside. Reinforce your table and supports so you do not overload it and risk collapse.

Depending on how close you are to ground zero, will allow you the amount of time you need to be inside and secured. The further away you are from ground zero the more time you have to get the last minute things done. Do what you can now to set up the fallout shelter. Now, if you do not have a basement or cellar, start thinking of sturdy, center and low interior rooms in your own home. Do the same type of barricading of mass on all the walls. Have your food and survival supplies readily available, placed just outside the door. Allow for bedding, sanitation and a cooking area.

What to Do *During* a Nuclear War or Event

Whatever the cause may be, let's say the worst happens and you hear on the radio that a nuclear device has exploded somewhere in the world. The popular belief that an astronomical amount of people will not survive a nuclear disaster is not true. The truth is that a majority of people will survive a nuclear detonation. The people and buildings in the immediate blast zone will not survive the explosion, but anyone who is still alive and uninjured after the explosion can stay alive *if* they get to a safe area that is protected against radioactive fallout. Do this list in order of importance. If time allows, start from the top of the list and work all the way down.

- Do not panic, think things through
- Gather your family together
- Be informed; Turn on a television or battery powered radio
- Take a thyroid blocking agent; Potassium Iodide - KI
- Go to the basement or lowest or center-most part of the house or building.
- Build a shelter if one does not already exist with close-by material
- Turn off the gas or propane and electricity and water
- Fill with water all tubs, basins, and empty containers with lids.
- Bring filled water containers and all non-perishable foods into your shelter enough for 3 weeks
- Bring clothing, bedding, and sanitary measures and supplies into your shelter
- Close and lock all windows and doors. Draw curtains and blinds
- Fill all basement window wells with sand, dirt, books, or any other dense material
- Cover chimneys and turn off air conditioners, vents, etc. to prevent fallout from coming inside
- Unplug *all* electric and electronic equipment including freezer

- Bring into your shelter an axe, pry-bars, and shovel in case you have to dig your way out
- Bring your Emergency Binder into the shelter
- Board up all windows and doors
- Prepare your house as you would for a tornado, hurricane or earthquake
- Cover all outside fuel sources (i.e. firewood, coal, etc.) with plastic or heavy canvas
- Secure all breakables, pictures, water heaters, china closets, vases, etc.
- Bring in or secure all lawn furniture, toys, and equipment.
- Fill all cars, trucks, ATV's, motorbikes, chainsaws, etc., with fuel.
- Move and lock up cars and trucks into garages, carports or other secured parking area
- Disconnect and remove the car battery, C.B. or HAM radios; *bring them inside.*
- Gather together all gardening supplies into one secure place.
- Cover all furniture, carpets, and rugs with plastic or dust cloths.
- Recheck food, water, sanitary supplies, bedding, and clothing in your shelter
- Do not bring pets into your own shelter or basement unless you have at least a three week food supply for them and proper sanitary measures.
- It is usually best to leave most pets and farm animals in a garage, shed, or barn with an ample supply of food and water. They have a tendency to survive radiation exposure much better than humans

Now, if the event is a nuclear meltdown and you live within the danger zone or downwind, you will be instructed by the authorities, to vacate the area.

Depending on the severity of the meltdown, the area will be uninhabitable for 50 to 200 years. With your Emergency Evacuation Plan, Binder, Emergency Car Kit and 72 hour Kit ready to go, you will be set to vacate far before everyone else.

When the event starts to unfold, people will start to panic. Telephone lines will be clogged as people immediately call loved ones then decide what to do. The internet will also be much busier, especially news sites, as people at work look for breaking information.

Upon a nuclear exchange or the beginning of a war, the stock market will crash creating tremendous economic disruption. Have cash available as the ATMs may not work or are empty. Roads will be packed. There may be lines or delays at gas stations. We will see empty shelves at the grocery store. Civil unrest will cause general lawlessness leaving the local police forces overwhelmed. Riots and looting, especially in densely populated urban areas, will certainly break out.

Once all your family members are at home, your key concerns will be protecting yourself and your loved ones from possible radiation, making sure you are safe from outside violence and lastly, you have enough supplies to live through the next few weeks or even months.

The supplies required for a lengthy stay in a fallout shelter are the same required for other disasters. Do not forget to take your 72-hour Kit, Car Kit, Emergency Binder, guns, ammo, sanitation supplies and all the food and water you can gather. The time is now that you and your family head down to the fallout shelter.

What to Do *After* a Nuclear Event

"How long do we stay inside?" Depending on the distance you are from ground zero and the size and location of the warheads will determine how long you need to stay inside the shelter. Listen to the battery powered radio to find out what kind of bomb was used and instructions on when it will be safe to exit your shelter.

It is recommended that if you are within the 350 mile downwind radius of an explosion that you stay indoors in a fallout shelter or basement shelter for at least two weeks and plan on sleeping in it for longer. After ten or so days you may venture out for a max of five minutes per day, increasing the amount of time you stay out each day by a few minutes; time needed to rid the shelter of waste and retrieve needed supplies.

If you are outside the 350 mile downwind radius of an explosion, stay indoors at least 7 to 8 days. The longer you are prepared to stay in the shelter, the safer you will be. After three weeks you will need to start your life over again.

Remember food production and water filtration should be top priority. The day to day job of living and surviving will then become a constant chore as food and supplies are scarce. Food and water are unaffected by direct radiation. However, they can still be contaminated by fallout particles. Exposed canned or bottled food items are safe and should be washed off before being opened and fallout-exposed solid foods can be eaten, but the outer ¼ inch should be peeled or cut off and disposed of after being washed off. While fallout-exposed porous foods, such as bread, should never be consumed.

Just as with any disaster, this event will take time and man power to repair the destroyed buildings, trade and commerce. The destruction and severity of the event will have a profound effect on the infrastructure of our society. A nuclear war will shatter the very foundation of this world as we know it; a catastrophic poisoning. The sheer size of the destruction, let alone the countless number of lives lost is mind boggling.

All of this is conjecture since we only have what has happened in the past to know how different societies would react. The earth is dynamic; it will repair itself and find balance. Throughout history mankind has bounced back from near extinction. With our survival know-how hard-wired into our very psychology we will again adapt, we will prevail and we will survive.

Acute Radiation Syndrome (ARS)

Acute radiation syndrome, or radiation sickness or poisoning is caused when a person receives a high dose of radiation within a few minutes. Radiation sickness is not contagious and exposure, like exposure to the sun, is cumulative. The most vulnerable to radiation poisoning are young children, elderly, and the sickly. The immediate symptoms of ARS are nausea, vomiting, and diarrhea. If the dose is high enough the sickness leads to bone marrow depletion, loss of appetite, infection, and bleeding. The survival rate depends on the radiation dose. For those who do survive, full recovery takes from a few weeks to 2 years. Keep hydrated and do not let the ill person be subjected to any more radiation.

Epidemics and Pandemics

The onset of a disease for a few people while contained and isolated would not be considered a pandemic. Just like a snow storm would need to meet certain criteria to be considered a blizzard; it is the same with a sickness or disease to be considered an epidemic. The difference between an epidemic and a pandemic is twofold; geographic spread and incidence rate.

An epidemic that is not contained to a city or a small area but covers a larger geographical area can be called a pandemic. An epidemic may be confined to a small area but affecting a very large amount of people. For example, a disease that has an expected rate of infection of 15% but reaches 40% of the population of a state, it is considered an epidemic. When 75% of the population is infected, it has then reached pandemic proportions.

An influenza pandemic occurs roughly three times a century. The most severe of the three was the influenza pandemic of 1918, known as the Spanish Flu which was caused by H1N1. It was said to originate in Asia but since it was reported by Spain, the name stuck. The Spanish Flu lasted from 1918 to 1919 and as in reported cases of the illnesses it comes in waves. Meaning the first initial wave of sick give it to the caretakers or others and then those give it to the third wave. What was so unusual about the Spanish Flu is that it killed healthy, young people. The total death toll worldwide was 50 million. Some would speculate it was more since record keeping of the day was not very accurate. The conditions in 1918 were not so far removed from the Black Death in the Middle Ages.

When H1N1 was first documented in Mexico in 2009, it was thought that the strain would reach the same severe pandemic level; as the death tolls were seeing healthy, young adults dying along with the elderly. The hyped sensationalism the news reported about the disease caused both panic and awareness, which may have lead to the eventual decline of spreading the disease.

The Asian flu in 1957 was caused by H2N2. Killing two million people, mostly children and elderly. The H3N2 flu pandemic was in 1968, mild by historical comparison, killing 33,800 people. Since 1997, CDC and others had been tracking a novel influenza, H5N1, called the bird flu which was and continues to be very deadly. About 60% of people who develop the illness die. The disease itself did not reach epidemic proportions.

While the awareness of germs and good hygiene around the world is at an all time high, which in fact, keeps diseases from reaching biblical proportions, it will not keep disease from starting or from evolving into a more serious and deadly strain.

The different strains of influenza adapt and mutate quicker than anti-biotics and anti-virals can be created. The over prescribing of anti-biotics has made our immune system incapable of fighting off these mutated resistant strains.

Some recent movies about the wide spread of disease are not far from the truth. The movie *Contagion* had CDC personal and epidemiologist on set to verify what would actually happen in the event of a pandemic today. The facts are real, reactions are speculative. There will be a lack of health care workers, medical supplies and workers who are either sick at home or are too afraid to go to work. Schools will be interrupted with the lack of teachers and bus drivers. Families will opt to keep their children home prior to any school officially closing. After a while there will be a shortage of coffins and morticians; massive death causes bodies to pile up as a result of an epidemic.

What you can do to protect yourself and your family is close to the same preparedness statute as other disaster/emergencies. Start with the knowledge that you will need to stay inside, stay healthy and away from crowds until the danger is over.

This is not like a nuclear event where you have to stay inside a shelter but you will have to *stay away* from people. Going outside is completely fine, but since you will not want to go to the store for your normal grocery shopping, you will need a large supply of food and water. The stores may not be open and gas stations may be empty from lack of workers filling the underground storage tanks.

It is also unknown if the electricity will be fully operational with a smaller work force overseeing the daily care. If the event gets bad enough that commerce is interrupted, then most things, if not everything, will come to a grinding halt. If you have to go out in public be mindful not to touch your face and it may be necessary to wear a facemask and gloves; if not mandated by the government then highly suggested.

Again, as with any other disaster/emergency have these needed items stocked in advance.

- Make sure you have enough food storage in place to last two to three months

- If electricity is out you will need a means of cooking your meals. A camp stove or gas grill will work nicely. Have plenty of extra fuel on hand
- You probably already have a well stocked water supply. Now add some variety like juice, soda, drink mixes, coffee, tea and electrolyte replacement drinks (see Homemade Pedialyte, Electrolyte Beverage in Chapter 6)
- You should have a two to three month supply of prescription medications and over the counter medications to help relieve the symptoms of the flu. Don't forget the vitamins.
- Stash a lot of soap and hand sanitizers. Use them often.
- Stock up on surgical masks and gloves, toilet paper, feminine products, all toiletries
- Hand-cranked or battery-powered radio or better yet flashlight-radio combinations that come with a hand crank to charge your cell phone
- Make sure you have a couple flashlights battery-powered lanterns and batteries
- Keep a well-stocked first aid kit close-by since minor ailments you will want to treat at home; the hospital is the last place you want to be during a pandemic.
- If you have children, plan some home schooling activities and some kind of entertainment

We will mourn and bury the dead. Work will resume. The flu will, in itself, die out, just as the other strands have in the past; usually after a few waves, the virus will lose its grip and the strong and prepared will survive.

Solar Flare and Magnetic Reversal

On Sept. 2, 1859, an extraordinary solar flare was witnessed by British astronomer Richard Carrington, an incredible storm of charged particles sent by the sun slammed into Earth's atmosphere the next day. The event, named the Carrington Event, produced vivid auroras in the night sky as far south as Cuba and Hawaii. Telegraph wires suddenly shorted out in the United States and Europe. Spark discharges shocked telegraph operators and set the telegraph paper on fire. Even when telegraphers disconnected the batteries powering the lines, aurora-induced electric currents in the wires still allowed messages to be transmitted. But other than that, life went on as normal.

The same would not be true if a major solar flare of similar size where to erupt today. We would be thrust back to the dark ages. Since our infrastructure is very dependent on electricity and electronics, our country would not fare well. A majority of electronic components and computers would cease to work. The large transformers would be fried leaving the power grid off-line, most of the cars and trucks with newer electronic systems will cease to work although cars and trucks older than 1970's would likely not be affected by the EMP wave.

The electrical grid will not get back on-line and have replacement parts for months, even years. This would collapse the transportation industry and commerce would come to a stop. Since the US is the bread basket of the world, third world nations would starve. The result would be millions of deaths from starvation and disease; a catastrophe the likes of which the world has never seen.

But how likely is a repeat of the Carrington Event? Scientists say it is not only possible; it is inevitable. What they do not know is *when* it will happen.

The sun operates on an 11-year cycle of activity. The next peak season is expected between 2012 and 2014. The best estimates suggest that super solar storms occur once every 100 years or so, which means we are 50 years overdue. The flare would need to be aimed right for the earth in order for it to be considered a threat.

The good news is that astronomers have the ability to forecast solar storms with some reliability, making the immediate call to shut down prime electronics prior to an EMP (electromagnetic pulse) hitting the earth. Also, the more advanced the technology and electronics get, the more they are hardened against an EMP wave.

Another doomsday hypothesis is pertaining to a geomagnetic flip. This suggestion mistakenly assumes that a pole reversal would momentarily leave the Earth without our magnetic field, which protects us from solar flares and coronal mass ejections from the sun. While Earth's magnetic field can be weak then strong at times, there is no indication that it has ever disappeared completely. A weaker field would lead to a small increase in solar radiation on Earth, which would create a beautiful display of aurora at lower latitudes, but nothing deadly.

According to the scientists of National Geographic and the British Geological Survey, a polar magnetic flip is not dangerous to life. Magnetic reversal or 'flip' is the process by which the North Pole is transformed into a South Pole and the South Pole becomes a North Pole.

A true reversal takes about a thousand years to complete, and during that time, contrary to popular belief, the magnetic field does not vanish. Interestingly, the magnetic field may sometimes only undergo an 'excursion', rather than a reversal. The compass will point a few degrees off of what we consider north but soon recharges itself back to where north is north and south is south.

Electromagnetic Pulse (EMP)

A major solar flare, coronal mass ejection (CME), a nuclear weapon detonation on the ground, or a high-altitude nuclear detonation in or above the earth's atmosphere (or E-Bomb) all create an electromagnetic pulse (EMP) , a high-density electrical field which acts like a stroke of lightning but is stronger and faster. EMP's have no direct effect on living things.

An electromagnetic pulse can seriously damage electronic devices connected to power sources or antennas, communication systems, computers, cell phones and cell towers, electrical appliances, automobile and aircraft ignition systems and the most threatening to our welfare is our electrical grid.

The United States has three electrical grids that supply the east, west and central continental states. If there is a shortage or electrical problem, the other grids can compensate by rerouting electricity to the needed area. But if a high altitude detonation (EMP) hits the central United States, all three grids will be compromised and lost. If two of the three grids are affected the third will not be able to compensate. The system will take months if not years to fix; creating a continuous blackout.

Both the EMP Commission and a 2008 study by the National Academy of Sciences (NAS) call for hardening the electrical grid and other components of the infrastructure to increase the chances they would survive, as well as creating a supply of spare parts of essential and complex components of the electrical grid infrastructure critical to communications.

The Scientific world has tried to bring attention to the solar storms, EMP and its dangers, though few have listened. But with the terrorist threat of a high altitude detonation creating a similar affect some have taken notice. The government has been advised on ways to protect or harden electronics from the EMP, but the cost is high. In comparison to the cost of repair and lives lost, the multi-million dollar price tag seems reasonable.

There are inexpensive ways for everyday people to protect smaller electronics from an electromagnetic pulse. Remember, this needs to be done prior to the pulse hitting the ground and we may or may not be told when that will occur. Unplug all electric and electronic equipment and disconnect all telephones, computer modems and any antenna that is taller than 12 feet; (12 feet antennas may be a thing of the past). Electronics plugged into a surge protector may save the equipment if the EMP is not so strong as to overpower it.

For smaller electronics, create a faraday cage by wrapping aluminum foil around a small cardboard box without any tears or holes, place cell phones or other important electronics inside an unwrapped box and place *that* box inside your new faraday cage. Make sure your electronics are not touching any metal lining. This simple box in a wrapped box will protect your small electronics completely.

Looters

After a disaster, the National Guard and the police will be called out, but they can't be everywhere at all times. Just as you assume responsibility for your own survival and protection you will have to protect your home and belongings from looters and home invaders.

The "looters will be shot" signs after Hurricanes were a deterrent against would-be looters. Sometimes just the threat will be all you need. Add spray paint to your survival list if this is something you wish to display.

But, there may come a time when you may have to make the ultimate survival decision and weigh the value of your life, or the life of your loved ones, against that of a criminal.

Alien Invasion

Lastly, alien invasion! Run and hide! Until you know their intentions, this seems to be the best advice. It will come out sooner or later that they have been here before and made contact with the government and authorities. "They" have helped with some of our most advanced air and spacecrafts through the efforts of reverse engineering. Any of the spacecrafts that have crashed landed in our borders are considered ours by default. Other countries have done the same thing with any aircrafts that may have crashed there.

The little gray ones with the huge eyes and the tall skinny ones that look more like a humanoid hybrid have made contact many times in the past.

Some alien theorists say that when they first showed up centuries ago the natives thought they were gods. The Native Americans called them Sky People. They said the sky people came from the sky to teach them a better way. All over the earth cultures have stated the sky people have taught their ancestors about math and astrology. And yes, they helped with the pyramids (on four continents). The Nezca lines in Peru, made all over the plains to be seen from the sky, were put there to beckon and welcome the sky people back, the stories and cave drawings, the stones in Puma Punku were cut with precision through advanced technology now lost.

There are countless mysteries that are explained away by assumptions. Everything that the ancient alien theorist believe to be true will soon be acknowledged as correct and that we have all been duped by the government for years.

…Or maybe not?

There is a lot of information out there. There are a lot of hoaxes, some real events and even more that cannot be explained. If you believe in extraterrestrial civilizations or not, the event may come when you will need to decide what *you* will do when or if they arrive. You can decide for yourselves.

"It is the mark of an educated mind to be able to entertain a thought without accepting it."
Aristotle *- 384 BC – 322 BC - Greek philosopher*

The End of Days???

What is the origin of the prediction the world will end in 2012?

The story started with a supposed planet discovered by the Sumerians in 4500 BC, called Nibiru. It was to have been on a 3600 year oval orbit around our sun and thus headed toward Earth. This catastrophe was initially predicted for May 2003, but when nothing happened, the doomsday date was moved forward.

Since the ancient Mayan calendar was to end the long cycle at the winter solstice in 2012 the two stories were linked to the end — hence the predicted doomsday date of December 21, 2012.

"It's the time when the largest grand cycle in the Mayan calendar — 1,872,000 days or 5,125.37 years — overturns and a new cycle begins," said Anthony Aveni, a Maya expert and archaeoastronomer at Colgate University in Hamilton, New York.

Just as our calendar does not cease to exist after December 31, the Mayan calendar does not cease to exist on December 21, 2012. Both continue and if your time is not up, you will continue also.

Another belief is in the existence of a huge, rouge planet Nibiru; this is not factual. The astronomers at NASA have found a plant on the outskirts of our solar system, which they named Eris. Eris is one of several *dwarf* planets, all of them on normal orbits that will never bring them near Earth. Like Pluto, Eris is smaller than our Moon. It is very far away, and its orbit never brings it closer than about 4 billion miles when it will be at its closest in the year 2055.

The *End of Days* predictions all have no basis of truth or fact; as the earth will not come to an abrupt end. With that said… the earth is still active with earthquakes and volcanoes, wildfires do start, and grand societies and cultures fall. Being prepared for something happening does not mean it will happen or that it is a desired event.

Y2K had a lot of hype but only in certain countries. Some grocery store shelves became empty. All that panic was caused by the possibility of a computer glitch that would throw the electrical grid off line. The hype did cause the government and large companies to fix the problem before it happened.

Now, multiply all that panic by *all* the nations in the world who have a belief the 'end is coming' at the end of 2012. December 21 rolled right into December 22, 2012, but the last minute panic may empty the grocery store shelves. Don't be left with nothing, stock up slowly now and you will not feel the need to get some last minute food when a disaster happens.

According to many religious beliefs, one day the world will cease to exist and the sun will not shine, but no one knows the hour nor the day (…not even the son; Matthew 24:36). Take care not to nurture fear. But also do not be lazy in thinking 'since nothing of that magnitude has happened before, it never will'.

Prepare yourself for the worst, hope for the best and pray. Realize there is an adventure out there called life; so live it to the fullest.

*"The fear of death follows from the fear of life. A man who lives fully is prepared to die at any time." - **Mark Twain***

Evacuation Grab List

In the case of disaster/emergency evacuation, split gathering list among adults and children to quicken the loading process

- Family Emergency Survival Book
- Full 72 Hour Emergency Car backpack in the car
- Emergency Binder with Important Documents
- Address phone book
- Computer and Photo back up on external drive, CD or Flash drive
- Gather flashlights, batteries, lantern and all candles
- Matches and lighters
- Gather all Food – Place cans and boxes in the bin/tote
- All baby food, toys and kids stuff
- Dog and/or cat food, water and toys
- All water containers - small containers can be bagged.
- Grab **all** Medicine, place in zip lock bag, grab trash bags and grocery bags
- Gather all camping gear
- All tools - shovel, axe, etc.
- Clothing: extra pair of everything including jackets and winter apparel
- Extras such as feminine products, shampoo, conditioner, etc.
- Bedding, Pillows and sleeping bags
- Place crow bar, fire extinguisher, fire arms, carrying case, ammo etc. under car seats

The camping gear tote/bin should have tents, stove, and fuel tanks, cooking utensils, tarp and rope. Place tarp over bin and tie down securely. Shut off utilities. Lock up house. Head for the hills!! Some of us are already here!

Emergency Binder

An emergency binder is a compilation of important papers and documents. In the event of an emergency, you can grab your binder and go. It is recommended storing your binder in a fireproof/ waterproof locked box or safe.

This should be small enough and light enough to be taken with you in an emergency. But if not, then open it and just take the binder. A 3 ring binder/folder with pockets and laminated or plastic page protectors works great. Copies and originals can be kept safe until needed. Here is a sample list of what you might want to keep secure. Again, add what is relevant to you in the space below.

- Cash and change – keep a variety of small bills on hand
- Birth Certificates
- Passports
- Vet records
- Social Security Cards
- Any work or tax documents difficult to replace
- Credit card bills with address and phone numbers
- Front and back copies of all your credit cards
- Life insurance policy
- Auto insurance policy
- Immunization records
- Homeowners insurance policy
- Bank account numbers and statements
- Retirement statements and portfolio
- All passwords (banking, internet sites, personal, etc)
- AAA / road assistance phone numbers and policy

Web sites to visit for more information

Please come visit my 'Survivaling' blog and 'Survival of the Prepared' websites:
http://www.lfwesseln.blogspot.com/
http://survivaloftheprepared.webstarts.com

For more information on disaster and emergency preparedness visit The American Red Cross Safe and Well Web site at
RedCross.org

For more information about radiation:
www.epa.gov/radiation
www.orau.gov/reacts/define.htm

Information on Protozoa check out the website -
http://www.answers.com/topic/protozoan#ixzz1pE2l h4D8

For more information pertaining to the earth, solar flares, magnetic poles and space visit
www.nasa.gov/topics/earth/features/2012.html
www.geomag.bgs.ac.uk/education/reversals.html
www.nasa.gov/

For info of the internal workings of the sun, check out: http://science.nasa.gov/heliophysics/

Interested in information about 'End of the World' myths go to
http://news.nationalgeographic.com/news/2009/11/09 1106-2012-end-of-world-myths.html

Tips on survival, as one of your sources for information go to - www.SurvivalNewsOnline.com

The National Gardening Association's web site is loaded with gardening tips - **http://www.garden.org/**

Interested in the Yellowstone Volcano information? Visit: **http://volcanoes.usgs.gov/yvo/**

To seek information on any topic visit **http://en.wikipedia.org/wiki/Main_Page**

Or just Google it!

(My personal favorite...)

Life isn't a journey to the grave arriving safely in a well preserved body, but rather to slide in sideways, chocolate in one hand, latte in the other, body thoroughly used up, totally worn out and screaming 'Woohoo What a ride'! -
Unknown

www.ingramcontent.com/pod-product-compliance
Lightning Source LLC
Chambersburg PA
CBHW070109290526
45789CB00005B/1977